D0626883

Four Dialectical Theories of Poetry

Four
Dialectical
Theories
of
Poetry

AN ASPECT OF ENGLISH
NEOCLASSICAL CRITICISM

Robert Marsh

THE UNIVERSITY OF CHICAGO PRESS
CHICAGO & LONDON

Standard Book Number: 226–50689–4

Library of Congress Catalog Card Number: 65–24432

THE UNIVERSITY OF CHICAGO PRESS, CHICAGO 60637
The University of Chicago Press, Ltd., London

Printed in the United States of America

to R. S. Crane

Preface

THIS IS AN ESSAY IN INTELLECTUAL HISTORY AND, CHIEFLY
by illustration, intellectual historiography. My primary purpose is to call attention to the existence and character of an
aspect of English criticism in the later seventeenth and eighteenth centuries—the "neoclassical" age, as it is often called—
that has largely been neglected in previous accounts of the
subject. It would be appropriate to consider the essay a supple-
ment in particular to two important articles by R. S. Crane,
"Neoclassical Criticism," first published in Joseph Shipley's
Dictionary of World Literature (1943), and "On Writing the
History of English Criticism, 1650–1800," published in the
University of Toronto Quarterly (July, 1953), and to the very
useful group of individual analyses by Walter J. Hipple entitled *The Beautiful, the Sublime, and the Picturesque in
Eighteenth-Century British Aesthetic Theory* (1957). They
employ methods of examining the critical discourse of the period broadly similar to mine but tend to leave what I have
called the "dialectical" tradition unexplored.

I have sought to perform the task by means of separate,
for the most part independent, examinations of the theories
of poetry produced by four writers who happen to illustrate
with unusual fullness the various special tendencies of dialectical criticism in the period. They are the philosopher–man-
of-taste A. A. Cooper, Third Earl of Shaftesbury; the phy-
sician-poet Mark Akenside; the physician-theologian David

Hartley; and the grammarian-philologian James Harris. The discussions of these theories constitute the four main chapters of the essay and are its primary burden. The opening chapter attempts to make clear the special sense in which the four theories may be viewed as representing a coherent aspect of the whole of neoclassical poetic theory and provides a general statement and justification of the basic principles and distinctions in terms of which the analyses in the main chapters are developed and organized and the summary observations in the concluding chapter are made.

My principal intention is thus to supply, with as little distortion as possible, some intelligible particulars that may prove useful for drawing a more complete picture of English neoclassical criticism than heretofore has been available. But I may be permitted a normal authorial belief that the significance of these particulars extends potentially beyond my immediate purpose. Although the four writers can scarcely be called major figures, either in the intrinsic excellence of their works or, with the possible exception of Shaftesbury, in the extent of their intellectual impact on their English contemporaries, they did enjoy considerable popularity on the Continent, especially in Germany, and were taken seriously by important writers in England in the nineteenth century, most notably by Samuel Taylor Coleridge. I think some new light may be shed here especially on the lines of continuity leading up to the poetic theories of the "Romantic" period, when so many of the major critics employed dialectical methods of one variety or another.

My explicit discussion of these matters, however, is meant only to be suggestive—to be of the nature, as it were, of what Coleridge himself called "aids to reflection"—and I have thought it best to present the discussion in an appendix to the main argument of the essay. Adequate exploration of such broader historical and practical kinds of significance would require a separate study of some magnitude and a method of comparative analysis rather different from the method employed in the bulk of this essay. Yet it would be a study which I think could not be properly conducted in the absence of the sort of materials this method is calculated to supply; and one of my aims has been to emphasize a kind of relationship between the formulation of larger historical comparisons and generalizations and the analysis of particular theories and systems in terms of their own special problems and modes of thought, a relationship that has not been very widely investigated in the recent historiography of ideas.

R. S. Crane kindly read the whole essay in manuscript and gave me the benefit of his wide knowledge of the history of criticism and his uniquely profound grasp of the problems and methods of intellectual history. Benjamin Sankey and Harold Zyskind also read parts of the essay in manuscript and made very valuable suggestions. In acknowledging the assistance of these friends I am not, I trust, implicating them in any of my errors or confusions. Portions of the chapters on Shaftesbury and Hartley were incorporated in the following published articles: "Shaftesbury's Theory of Poetry: The Importance of the 'Inward Colloquy,' " *ELH*, XXVIII, No. 1 (March, 1961), 54–69; "The Second Part of Hartley's System," *Journal of the History of Ideas*, XX, No. 2 (April, 1959), 264–73; and "Mechanism and Prescription in David Hartley's Theory of Poetry," *The Journal of Aesthetics and Art Criticism*, XVII, No. 4 (June, 1959), 473–85. I am grateful to the publishers of those journals for permission to reprint the materials here.

ROBERT MARSH

Huntington, New York
March 1, 1965

Contents

xi

NEYTHER LET IT BE DEEMED TOO SAWCIE A COMPARISON TO ballance the highest poynt of mans wit with the efficacie of Nature: but rather give right honor to the heavenly Maker of that maker: who having made man to his owne likenes, set him beyond and over all the workes of that second nature, which in nothing hee sheweth so much as in Poetrie: when with the force of a divine breath, he bringeth things forth far surpassing her dooings, with no small argument to the incredulous of that first accursed fall of *Adam:* sith our erected wit, maketh us know what perfection is, and yet our infected will, keepeth us from reaching unto it.

SIR PHILIP SIDNEY, Apologie for Poetrie

THE DIVINITY IS A BOUNDLESS OCEAN OF BLISS AND GLORY: Human minds are smaller streams, which, arising at first from the ocean, seek still, amid all their wandrings, to return to it, and to lose themselves in that immensity of perfection.

IN THE TRUE SAGE AND PATRIOT ARE UNITED WHATEVER can distinguish human nature, or elevate mortal man to a resemblance with the divinity. The softest benevolence, the most undaunted resolution, the tenderest sentiments, the most sublime love of virtue, all these animate successively his transported bosom.

DAVID HUME, "The Platonist" and "The Stoic"

AND BLEST ARE THEY,
Who in this fleshly World, the elect of Heaven,
Their strong eye darting through the deeds of men,
Adore with steadfast unpresuming gaze
Him Nature's essence, mind, and energy!

S. T. COLERIDGE, "Religious Musings"

⊰ 1 ⊱

Forms of Neoclassical Theory

THE SUBJECT OF THIS ESSAY IS THE "DIALECTICAL" tradition in English criticism from about 1650 to about 1800. What that was, precisely, and how it ought to be examined may best be understood in the context of a preliminary outline of the critical thought of the period as a whole, because the very existence of the tradition, so to speak, depends on a rather special view of the various materials of that whole. It will be most convenient to attempt this in relation to a single, but clearly universal, critical topic such as the nature and value of poetry, and it is important to extend the outline to Europe in general because of the great amount of intellectual "cross-fertilization" that took place among the major nations.

Even when limited to poetic theory, this is not a routine task. The total body of theorizing about poetry in this period presents a massive and complex spectacle of diversity, conflicts, and combinations of special definitions, problems, procedures, and doctrines, and it often seems to defy perception of any meaningful order that is not a distortion or deliberate oversimplification for special polemic purposes. Some scholars, assuming in general the existence and determinative priority of coherent, theoretically unified episodes in intellectual history (as if ages rather than men produce ideas), have looked for a central core of specific principles or doctrines necessarily shared by neoclassical theorists; [1] they have found only some

---

[1] See, e.g., W. K. Wimsatt, Jr. and Cleanth Brooks, *Literary Criticism: A Short History* (New York, 1957), pp. 174–279. Cf. J. W. H. Atkins, *English Literary Criticism: 17th and 18th Centuries* (London, 1951), *passim*.

commonplace formulas such as "imitation of nature," "delight and profit," and *ut pictura poesis,* which could have no very specific meaning at all when attributed to the whole period (except by the arbitrary decision of the scholar himself) even if they happened to be in fact universal features of neoclassical criticism. Other scholars, recognizing and facing up to the manifest plurality of specific principles and doctrines, have settled for the general coherence that may indeed be found in the critical language of the period.[2] But most of them would probably agree that it is not reasonable to speak of a unified neoclassical age of *theory* only on the basis of a loose, somewhat amorphous collection of terms and oppositions of terms which critics employed in common. Valuable as it is for acquiring a sense of the general discursive flavor of the period, the identification of such a body of commonplaces and characteristic "metaphors" (however different it might have been from that of another period) provides at best a material coherence; and where the special meanings—"denotations" as well as "connotations"—of such key terms vary radically and often, as they obviously did, it is a material coherence of probably the least important kind.

Conceivably, however, we can find a useful organization for the actual theorizing of the neoclassical period (without necessarily distorting or oversimplifying the primary data) if we give up, or at least postpone for a time, the search for a real unity of specific principles and doctrines, and if we venture to move beyond the consideration of the material causes to an examination of the human "formative causes" of theory—that is, the special theoretical problems taken seriously by different writers and the methods employed to solve them. This prob-

---

2 See, e.g., M. H. Abrams, *The Mirror and the Lamp* (New York, 1953), pp. 30–69, 184–213; cf. R. S. Crane, "On Writing the History of English Criticism, 1650–1800," *University of Toronto Quarterly,* XII (1953), 384–86. See George Boas, *The Limits of Reason* (New York, 1961), pp. 71–99, for a recent statement of the rationale of the "basic metaphor" approach to intellectual history.

lematic approach (as it may be called) implies the belief that real intellectual characteristics frequently exist in an unstable and unpredictable relation to the commonplace verbal elements and structures in which they may be found; and this reflects the further assumption (which cannot be "proved" any more easily than it can be "refuted") that the "theories" which we seek to examine and understand are the products of individual human intellectual *actions,* not of "natural processes," divine providence, general linguistic development, or racial myth. In other words, what produces a theory out of a man's nature and experience, his reading of other writers, and in general his conceptual and linguistic equipment is his personal recognition and definition of a set of intellectual problems that are important to him and his attempt to solve them by whatever means seem to him appropriate or necessary. Were it not for this formative action, no theories about any subject would ever come into existence, although some of the potential *materials* of theory might exist.[3]

Necessarily, of course, even the problematic historian must discuss theories in terms of characteristics which two or more human beings may be said to have in common if he wishes to say something at least potentially intelligible; individuality *as such* is intellectually inaccessible. The following outline of

---

[3] The principal focus here is not, however, on different neoclassical attempts to solve those very general critical problems which Crane has distinguished—"technical," "qualitative," and "circumstantial" (*op. cit.,* pp. 386–90). Such categories are theoretically neutral; they are quite useful for classifying individual arguments and theories in terms of the *common* general concerns of literary history and criticism, but they have limited value for understanding the various special theoretical schemes in which critical problems are actually formulated and solved. When, moreover, the historian's interest is particularly the differentiation of theories of the nature and value of poetry, the kinds of problems which he must take as his primary subject are inevitably more narrowly specified; for here he must be deliberately concerned to isolate peculiar problems which reflect the different kinds of theoretical principles and modes of thought about the subject rather than simply the general problems common to different theoretical positions.

neoclassical poetic theory thus presents distinctions not of theories but of forms of theory—of the basic *kinds* of problems and methods of reasoning or inquiry in terms of which writers in this period gave special meaning and value to the materials of commonplace terminology and critical formulas available to them for the construction of theories. They may be called forms of "neoclassical" theory with special appropriateness because they have been generalized in part from the writings of critics and philosophers of classical antiquity. They are particularly useful to the historian of neoclassical poetics because they provide, in specifically formative intellectual terms, frameworks within which individual theories and groups of theories may be made intelligible systematically as productions belonging not only to coherent parts or aspects of a special historical whole but also to a larger context of human intellectual activity in general.

PROBLEMATIC, RHETORICAL, AND CAUSAL FORMS

One of the forms of theory, found in antiquity in the *Poetics* of Aristotle, may itself be given the name "problematic." [4]

---

[4] I am aware of the slight rhetorical awkwardness here in using the label "problematic" for the method of this essay and for one of the forms of poetic theory, but it would be misleading to use different names for them, since the basic difference is only one of immediate subject matter, not of orientation, purpose, and mode of reasoning.

In distinguishing and naming these forms of theory my primary debt is to the writings of Richard McKeon, especially his long essay "Imitation and Poetry," in *Thought, Action, and Passion* (Chicago, 1954), pp. 102–221. Unless I have misunderstood him, however, McKeon's own subject matter, purpose, and method in that work are quite different from mine, and I have no evidence that he ever intended the distinctions to be used as I have used them here. It should be understood, moreover, that McKeon cannot be held in any way responsible for the lists of particular neoclassical writers and works which I supply as examples under the four headings. It will perhaps be noticed that the present distinctions bear some general similarities also to those presented by Stephen C. Pepper in *The Basis*

The primary concern is to distinguish, inductively and in literal terms, the special problems of human art, or "making," in its various kinds from those of social action and scientific or philosophical knowledge, and to isolate the different principles governing the performance of basic kinds of literary tasks (of which, in Aristotle's own analysis, there appear to be four: poetry, rhetoric, history, and philosophy or science). The problematic theorist, in other words, while not assuming the one universal nature and purpose of all things that happen to be called poems, approaches the subject of poetry as such from the point of view of distinguishing the peculiar problems which poets alone have to solve, as well as the peculiar problems of writing poems in the different species, or forms, that have been produced.

Instances of this kind of inquiry have not been plentiful in any age, but analogues and hints can often be found. In the neoclassical period, Thomas Hobbes, for example, in his "Answer to D'Avenant's preface before Gondibert" (1650), makes use of distinctions, between "poetry" and "verse," and among philosophy, history, and poetry, which suggest the method of Aristotle. Hume and Kant, like Aristotle, thought it important to distinguish the general problems of criticism or aesthetics from those of ethics and of knowledge. However, among the direct treatments of poetry, or of what we have come to call imaginative literature, only Henry Fielding's prefaces to *Joseph Andrews* (1742) and to Sarah Fielding's *The Adventures of David Simple* (1744) and Lessing's *Laokoon* (1766) and *Hamburgische Dramaturgie* (1767–69) provide relatively clear examples of the problematic approach, and these works actually confront a rather limited number of different literary problems.[5] There were, of course, throughout the Renaissance

---

of *Criticism in the Arts* (Cambridge, Mass., 1945) and in *World Hypotheses* (Berkeley and Los Angeles, 1942).

[5] For a perceptive and closely reasoned analysis of Fielding's preface to *Joseph Andrews,* and an account of some of the corroborative evidence in

and seventeenth and eighteenth centuries, numerous "Aristotelian," and anti-"Aristotelian," discussions of the rules and
species of poetry. But what passed commonly for Aristotle in
the vast majority of these discussions were isolated terms and
statements from the *Poetics* assimilated to kinds of theory
which Aristotle either had taken pains to refute or had assigned to branches of learning other than the productive
sciences or arts of *poesis*. In general, truly problematic, differential methods of analysis of the sort employed by Aristotle
were scarce indeed.

There were many instances, however, of a mode of discussion which Aristotle himself perhaps would have called "rhetorical" (and for which his own *Rhetoric* was one of the earliest
sources of topics and distinctions). It is a mode in which the
works of poets are treated as means rather than ends, and as
means in particular of achieving special socially determined
ends. Thus different species of poems, for example, are not
viewed (as they are in the *Poetics*) as possible unique problems
of artistic construction, differentiated inductively according
to an empirical grasp of the different principles of their constitution. They are viewed, rather (as in Horace's *Ars poetica*),
as more or less conventional, prescribed modes of communica-
tive discourse or affective composition, through which certain
pre-established effects or literary qualities can be achieved.
And they are differentiated, in an essentially deductive manner (much as Aristotle differentiates the materials of persua-

---

his preface to *David Simple,* see Homer Goldberg, "Comic Prose Epic or
Comic Romance: The Argument of the Preface to *Joseph Andrews,*" *Philological Quarterly,* XLIII (1964), 193–215. For detailed explanation and
justification of this interpretation of Aristotle (with minor variations), see
McKeon, "Aristotle's Conception of Language and the Arts of Language,"
in *Critics and Criticism, Ancient and Modern,* ed. R. S. Crane (Chicago,
1952), pp. 176–231; Elder Olson, "The Poetic Method of Aristotle: Its
Powers and Limitations," *English Institute Essays, 1951* (New York, 1952),
pp. 70–94; Crane, *The Languages of Criticism and the Structure of Poetry*
(Toronto, 1953), pp. 39–79.

sion in the *Rhetoric*), according to the special endowment and training of the poet and the special demands of subject matter and method made by different audiences.

This was the basic approach of the major practical critics in England—Dryden, Pope, and Johnson. It was, indeed, the most common neoclassical approach, particularly in the first half of the period, throughout Europe. A primary concern with species of poems, rather than with general "qualities" of writing, was not universal, but a clear majority of neoclassical critics shared the habit of viewing poets and poetry, both ancient and modern, in terms of the special problems of producing and controlling (by "art" and "nature") the kinds and qualities of subject matter, arrangement, and style determined a priori to be necessary or appropriate to the audience or the established norms of the art. And, in spite of the popularity of terms and statements of doctrine which had their origins in essentially non rhetorical treatises, including especially Aristotle's *Poetics* and the *Peri hypsous* of "Longinus," [6] the governing topics and principles came chiefly from the social rhetorics of Cicero and Quintilian and from rhetorically oriented literary handbooks like those of Horace, Dionysius of Halicarnassus, and Demetrius.

Moreover, although the number of critics having the limited pragmatic, technical orientation common among the rhetoricians gradually diminished in the eighteenth century, the tradition of classical rhetoric and rhetorically oriented poetics

---

6 The *Peri hypsous* offers an unusual case. Although neoclassical writers generally failed to realize the difference (just as they had little trouble combining Horace and Aristotle), the main principles and doctrines of the treatise are not rhetorical in the sense in which those of Horace or Cicero are. A large proportion of its terms are derived from the tradition of classical rhetoric, but Longinus distinguishes the "sublime" from ordinary rhetorical effectiveness or excellence, as well as from truth and structural beauty, and thus in a general sense his approach perhaps may best be viewed as problematic, although, unlike Aristotle, he is concerned directly with the problems of achieving a special quality of discourse, not with distinguishing the problems special to various literary forms.

remained dominant in the body of critical terms and distinctions characteristic of the period.[7] Few neoclassical critics, of whatever theoretical persuasion, were willing to dispense entirely with such familiar elements of critical vocabulary as (to give a sampling from the French) *plaisir* and *profit, invention, sublimité* or *grandeur, propriété* or *decorum, goût, esprit* or *génie* and *jugement* or *bon sens* (common translations of Horace's *ingenium* and *sapere* [*sapientia*]), and *imitation* (in the sense of copying or emulating or "following" ancient and modern masters and models—the principal meaning which the term had for Isocrates, Cicero, and Quintilian, as well as for Horace).[8]

Nor was the use of the commonplaces of classical rhetoric limited to discussions of poems and poets; it was extended throughout the period to the comparison of poetry and other arts and even to systems of general aesthetics. Dryden, for example, used the familiar Ciceronian concepts "invention," "disposition," and "expression" to organize his "Parallel betwixt Poetry and Painting" (1695). Baumgarten depended, in his *Meditationes philosophicae de nonnullis ad poema pertinentibus* (1735) and in his *Aesthetica* (1750–58), on the three styles of oratory distinguished by Cicero—plain, medium, and sublime—as well as on the "ut pictura poesis" principle of Horace and Simonides of Ceos, in developing his conceptions of poetry as "sensate discourse" and aesthetics as the study of "sensitive cognition."

---

[7] See the article by Crane cited above in note 2 for a useful summary list of the characteristic terms in the critical "language" of the period in England.
[8] Even such supposedly modern notions as the *je ne sais quoi* of Père Bouhours's *Entretiens d'Ariste et d'Eugène* (1671) and the "grace beyond the reach of art" of Pope's *Essay on Criticism* can be traced at least as far back as Quintilian's *quidquid arte non traditur* (*Instititio oratoria* X. ii. 12). Cf. also the "elevation of genius which can never be produced by any art or study" of William Temple's essay "Upon Poetry" (1690) and the *no sé qué* of B. J. Feijóo's *Teatro crítico universal* (1726–41). See Samuel H. Monk, " 'A Grace Beyond the Reach of Art,' " *Journal of the History of Ideas*, V (1944), 131–50.

Obviously, however, use of the traditional language of rhetoric does not necessarily mean adherence to the special kinds of principles, issues, and procedures found among rhetoricians and rhetorically minded critics. A third kind of theory, which perhaps may best be called "causal," was developed early in the period and eventually became one of the principal modes of discussing art and literature. It is a "neoclassical" kind of theory in the sense that the basic attitude and mode of reasoning, though not essentially characteristic of any of the literary critics of antiquity, do go back to the philosophical tradition of Leucippus, Democritus, Epicurus, and Lucretius. It is causal theory in the sense that the central consideration is not how best to *obtain* predetermined literary qualities or effects but rather how to *explain* qualities and effects in relation to the natural behavior of human beings. Poetry is discussed not primarily in terms of established techniques or criteria of expression or of a general analogy to social action (although the results of the behavioral analysis can provide answers to technical and practical questions), but in terms of natural causes. In the neoclassical period this was usually done by means of principles and methods derived from various empiricist systems of epistemology, psychology, and "natural philosophy." [9] Although concepts were adopted freely

---

[9] This is the tradition on which W. J. Hipple's *The Beautiful, the Sublime, and the Picturesque in Eighteenth-Century British Aesthetic Theory* (Carbondale, Ill., 1957) tends to concentrate, although Hipple is not concerned specifically with the theories of poetry formulated in this mode, and he includes two aestheticians (Reynolds and Alison) having marked dialectical inclinations. Obviously the way for this general causal approach was prepared by the writings of Bacon, Galileo, Descartes, Robert Boyle, Gassendi, Glanvill, Hobbes, Locke, and Newton, but in explaining its rise to prominence in the eighteenth century one would probably have to consider also the various historical accounts of the Epicurean philosophy, as in Thomas Stanley's *History of Philosophy* (1655–62), the direct use of Lucretius' *De rerum natura,* and the tinctures and suggestions of causal methods discoverable in the works of the more popular ancient critics—as in the *Poetics* (4. 1448b4–1449a7), the *Ars poetica* (180–88), Plutarch's *Moralia* (17F–18B), and the *Peri hypsous* (xxii. 1; xliv. 1–11).

from rhetorical and other traditions (as in the wide use of "sublimity" and "novelty," or the Aristotelian-Horatian distinctions of genres), they were always given special meanings and status by the requirement that aesthetic faculties, forms, and qualities be deduced from a prior analysis of natural human behavior. And that analysis commonly involved systematic treatment of the simple causal elements of human thought and feeling (vibrations, sensations, simple ideas, impressions), their natural loci (pleasures and pains, tastes, inner senses, habits), and their essentially mechanical principles of organization (association, imitation, concatenation).

In the early years of the period (as in some of the writings of Saint-Évremond, Huet, Bouhours, Fontenelle, Temple, and Dennis), this mode of analysis took chiefly the special, somewhat less systematic, historical form of a search for the natural causes of individual and "national" differences of subject matter, manner, and style among poets and their works.[10] As a special type of neoclassical aesthetics and literary theory (as distinct from history) the causal-empirical approach had its main systematic beginnings in Addison's *Spectator* papers on "The Pleasures of the Imagination" (1712). Important works to follow included the Abbé du Bos's *Réflexions critiques sur la poésie et sur la peinture* (1719), Francis Hutcheson's *Inquiry into the Original of our Ideas of Beauty and Virtue* (1725), Hume's essays "Of Tragedy" and "Of the Standard of Taste" (1757), treatises and essays by Montesquieu, Burke, Alexander

---

10 Whereas the normal procedure in rhetorical methods was to explain such differences on the basis of varying rhetorical circumstances (gifts, education, and special audiences), the causal historian did so on the basis of the environmental conditions (social structure, language, climate, soil, terrain) which, according to the universal laws of human psychology and physiology, could cause such differences of behavior. This interest in the "natural" laws of historical causation was more fully developed in later comparisons and formal histories of the poetry of different ages and societies. On this movement see René Wellek, *The Rise of English Literary History* (Chapel Hill, 1941), especially for a useful list of primary references.

Gerard, Adam Smith, Lord Kames, George Campbell, J. G. Sulzer, Cesare Beccaria, and some of the works of Thomas Reid and his followers, among many others. By the last quarter of the eighteenth century, causal analysis, frequently called "philosophical criticism," was a very popular mode of discussing literary subjects.

THE DIALECTICAL FORM: ORIENTATION, METHOD, THEMES

The rhetorical and the causal forms of theory were clearly the predominant ones in the neoclassical period, but they were not without the companionship of a more transcendental and metaphysical form. A number of writers produced theories of poetry of a kind whose main characteristics go back primarily to Plato, the Stoics, and the Neoplatonists but which perhaps are best called "dialectical" to avoid suggesting that they are peculiar to any one doctrinal school or tradition. Dialectical theories differ radically from problematic and causal theories in that the dialectician discusses poetry (and most other things as well) primarily by means of broad analogies and syntheses, rather than by literal differentiation and analysis, and he does so within the context of a controlling a priori disjunction or opposition between two realms or conceptions of the whole of things—the higher or better ultimate reality and the lower "sublunary," "merely human," or "common" world. Hence they differ also from rhetorical theories, whose methods commonly involve an analogy to social action and the use of better-worse distinctions, in going beyond the standards and problems of accommodating particular audiences and societies. The dialectical theorist, in other words, invokes transcendent or comprehensive values, patterns, and ideals for poetry that are said to reside in God himself, or to exist in a providential emanating system of spiritual essences, or to be embodied in nature, mind, language, or history—or some kind of combination or fusion of these. And, methodologically, he justifies the application of such criteria by his characteristic dialectical habit of perceiving the patterns of similitude, congeniality, or continuity between the "ultimate" and the "common." Poetry is thus discussed not primarily in terms of unique problems of human artistic construction, or of artistic conventions, conditions, or techniques and their immediate social effectiveness (although such matters may be included), or in terms of natural psychological or physical causes and effects (although such an inquiry may accompany or be assimilated to the higher considerations), but rather in terms of the apprehension, expression, or creation of some kind of supreme or transcendent reality and order.

It happens, however, that dialectical theories are not always easy to distinguish in a predominantly non-dialectical age unless a special effort is made to give the dimensions of basic problems and method general analytical precedence over terminology and statements of doctrine, because the dialectical theorist need not confine himself to peculiarly Platonic, Stoic, or Neoplatonic terms and ideas. He can always recognize, incorporate, and even make extensive positive use of principles and concepts originally derived from problematic, rhetorical, and causal theories. The test is whether he insists on bringing such materials finally (in one manner or another) within a framework of superior values and meanings by virtue of which it is possible to transcend or properly control the supposedly inferior or incomplete sublunary and merely human levels on which critics taking those rival approaches characteristically operate.

The importance, of course, of the tradition of Platonism in the history of dialectical poetic theory can scarcely be overemphasized, and it is not wholly an indulgence in historical analogies to say that in dialectical theories the poet and his performance are commonly defined and evaluated by reference (positive or negative—or paradoxical) to the nature and power of a special quasi-Platonic dialectician-lawgiver (human or divine), daimon, or demiurge—or all three. In any case, these have been the recurrent themes of dialectical poetics up to our own day: knowledge, or simply apprehension, of the "true" scheme of things (and the special social value of such knowledge or apprehension); inspiration or enthusiasm (particularly in relation to the "non-artistic" or unlearnable aspects of human poetic production); and resemblance to divine art or creativity. For these are the three principal ways in which human mind and action can be related to the substances and structure of *ultimate* reality. Hence it is in large part on the basis of their consideration and special treatment of one or more of these themes, whether or not they overtly identify them with Plato, that dialectical theories of poetry may be distinguished from non-dialectical theories, in any period of history.

The writings of the Third Earl of Shaftesbury, Mark Akenside, David Hartley, and James Harris offer unusually instructive instances of dialectical theory in English neoclassical criticism: they provide more or less detailed and coherent accounts of poetry and the poet and employ all three of the common dialectical themes, directly or indirectly, in doing so.[11]

---

[11] It should be noted, however, that there were other substantial works produced in which dialectical principles and procedures of one sort or another tend to control the discussion of poetry, including, for example, Thomas Rymer's *Tragedies of the Last Age Considered* (1678), Jeremy Collier's *Short View of the Immorality and Profaneness of the English Stage* (1698), Dennis' *The Grounds of Criticism in Poetry* (1704), William Law's *Absolute Unlawfulness of the Stage-Entertainment* (1726), Vico's *Principii d'una scienza nuova* (1725–44), J. C. Hamann's *Kreuzzüge des Philologen* (1762), and Herder's *Vom Geist der Ebräischen Poesie* (1783); and there were many less fully developed and less systematic instances throughout the period (particularly among the poets themselves), in England and on the Continent, of the application of transcendental or comprehensive moral-religious criteria as the true test of poetic value. See, e.g., William Davenant's Preface to *Gondibert* (1650), Isaac Watts's Preface to *Horae Lyricae* (1706), James Thomson's Preface to the second edition of *Winter* (1726), Joseph Warton's "Ode to Fancy" (1746) and

Moreover, they are especially representative neoclassical theories because in developing their accounts of poetry they drew heavily not only from the traditions of Platonism and Stoicism and certain later dialectical systems of general philosophy, especially those of Descartes, Malebranche, and Leibniz, but also from various instances of the three kinds of non-dialectical theory discoverable in the period. The more familiar terms and topics of classical rhetoric and rhetorical poetics are found in the works of all four writers. Problems and ideas taken from the *Poetics* of Aristotle and from empiricist philosophies (including those of Democritus, Epicurus, and Lucretius themselves, as well as Newton and Locke) are also employed, both positively and negatively, and in varying amounts, as materials to be shaped and purified according to the dialectical ideals. None of the four writers could reasonably be called a major figure; but all reveal the power of the dialectical approach, even when it is pursued by men of less than pre-eminent rank in thoroughness and subtlety, to avoid or overcome the obstacles which non-dialectical philosophies seem to place in the way of the comprehensive and absolute truth. Collectively, they may perhaps be viewed as offering something approximating the range of subjects, interests, and philosophical implications of a major dialectical thinker such as Plato, Augustine, or Spinoza.

William Collins' "Ode on the Poetical Character" (1747). For useful discussions, though chiefly in doctrinal terms, of the historical development and significance of different general aspects of this tradition see Oskar Walzel, *Das Prometheussymbol von Shaftesbury zu Goethe* (2nd ed.; Munich, 1932); Margaret Sherwood, *Undercurrents of Influence in English Romantic Poetry* (Cambridge, Mass., 1934), pp. 3–147; Ernst Cassirer, *The Platonic Renaissance in England*, trans. James P. Pettegrove (Austin, Tex., 1953), pp. 157–202; Earl Wasserman, "Nature Moralized: The Divine Analogy in the Eighteenth Century," *ELH*, XX (1953), 39–76; M. H. Abrams, "The Correspondent Breeze: A Romantic Metaphor," *Kenyon Review*, XIX (1957), 113–30.

THE ANALYSIS OF INDIVIDUAL THEORIES

The general characteristics of the dialectical mode of thought, abstracted from the collection of particular arguments and theories in which they are initially perceived as common, can be stated summarily: the fundamental problem is to grasp the harmony, parallel, or identity between the forms or processes of human life and those of true or ultimate reality. In solving this problem the dialectician gives logical and conceptual priority to the exhaustive disjunction or opposition between the better and the worse parts or conceptions of the whole things, and he makes progress in inference and discourse primarily by perceiving lines of analogy and means of synthesis rather than by literal differentiation and analysis. But this is necessarily a neutral description within the range of the dialectical mode itself, serving only to distinguish it broadly from other modes. The special dialectical principles, issues, and procedures of Shaftesbury, Akenside, Hartley, and Harris not only differ as a group from those ordinarily found among dialecticians in other periods but also differ from each other in important ways which the historian must not obscure. Similarly, the three common themes of dialectical poetics are semantically and doctrinally neutral within the total scope of the dialectical approach. They are singularly appropriate for organizing the analysis of a group of particular theories, but in this use they do not signify special principles or doctrines; they are rather like "second intention" concepts, merely indicating general areas of interest or concern which men, especially those with dialectical inclinations, have from time to time taken seriously, in their own particular terms and definitions and in various relations to other philosophical and critical topics, as means of determining and discussing the nature and value of poetry. Individual writers' concern with comprehensive dialectical oppositions and their resolution and with the questions of poetic knowledge, inspiration, and

creative power will always be made conceptually specific and
given actual theoretical significance in their own special con-
texts—their own special decisions as to what the ultimate
sources of value are, what the poet really is and does (thus
what "poetry" really means) and hence what commonplace
topics of criticism must be taken most seriously, and what peculiar procedures of thought and discussion can or ought to
be employed in treating these and like matters.

One point, therefore, should be given special emphasis. The
dialectical aspect of neoclassical poetic theory does not consist
of a system of specific principles and doctrines or "opinions,"
or only of a special kind of critical language and subject matter, shared by certain writers. Such are the characteristics of
theories to which historians of criticism have ordinarily confined their attention (and there is no reason why anyone
should not continue to do so if these are the characteristics
which interest him); but the concern here is with something different: a general kind of theoretical orientation and
method, within whose legitimate scope numerous special conceptual and doctrinal differences, and even oppositions, concerning questions of poetry and the poet are possible.

This does not mean, of course, that the four writers cannot
share any really identical intellectual problems of a specific
sort. It does mean that to present their theories a priori as
variant solutions of a special identical problem (or related set
of problems), however valuable this might be for poetic, social, or even philosophical purposes, would be to run the
unnecessary risk of confusing "regulative ideas" with "constitutive principles," as Kant termed them,[12] and thus to encourage historically insidious analogies among the theories, if not
simple distortions. For it would demand a common descrip-

---

12 See *Critique of Pure Reason,* Appendix to Chap. III, Section vii, of
"Transcendental Dialectic": "Of the Regulative Employment of the Ideas
of Pure Reason." The immediate application is different, but the general
distinction is, I think, essentially the same.

tive terminology and a continuing process of overt comparison in severe abstraction from the concrete details of the individual writers' actual efforts. If only for practical reasons, then, the discussion of any specific identities of problem and solution that might exist among the four theories, or between them and dialectical theories of other periods, ought to follow upon, and derive from, independent accounts of the four writers' own peculiarities of immediate purpose, conception, procedure, and argument—insofar as those peculiarities may be rendered generally intelligible. If theories are indeed produced by individual human beings, surely there is nothing to fear in this approach.

⊰ 2 ⊱

Shaftesbury and the Inward
Colloquy

THAT THE THIRD EARL OF SHAFTESBURY SHOULD BE
identified with the general tradition of Platonism, and not
with the empirical tradition of Hobbes and Locke, has become
rather common knowledge and requires no special demonstra-
tion here. Probably the most widely known element of his
philosophy is his conception of inner senses, the innate mental forms of natural affection and taste, upon which he based
his discussion of ethical and aesthetic matters. It is generally
recognized that Shaftesbury viewed these inner senses not as
actual perfections of soul but as "predispositions" or "precon-
ceptions" which may be corrupted by the seductive power of
custom and fashion unless they are developed and controlled
according to the "just standard of nature."[1] But it seems not
to be generally recognized that, for the task of developing and
controlling them, thus giving them practical philosophical and
social significance, he attached great importance to a method
of self-examination and criticism by "inward colloquy" or
"soliloquy" through which a man may successfully rebuff the

---

[1] *Soliloquy; Or Advice to an Author,* III. 3, in *Characteristics of Men, Manners, Opinions, Times, etc.,* ed. John M. Robertson (London, 1900), I, 228.
Cf. "Miscellaneous Reflections," III. 2, *ibid.,* II, 257. Hereafter, in references to Shaftesbury's *Characteristics,* numerals in parenthesis (or in square
brackets) indicate volume and page of this edition.

corrupting advances of custom and fashion.[2] The common view appears to be that he was espousing an almost primitivistic intuitionism in which the proper development of the inner senses is said to be effected, curiously enough, simply by "following" the dictates of those very predispositions. As one scholar has put it, "Nature herself directs the way, and to be good man needs only to obey his natural instinct."[3] The fact is, however, that Shaftesbury saw the task of obeying one's proper natural instinct as requiring a laborious preliminary inner struggle of the mind. The process is, as he says, "wholly

---

2 Reference to the "soliloquy" and to Shaftesbury's interest in the concept and process of "self-examination" is made by Ernest Tuveson in his interesting article "The Importance of Shaftesbury," *ELH*, XX (1953), 267–99; see esp. pp. 289–290. For Tuveson, however, this is simply one of a number of ways in which Shaftesbury expresses his notion of the "necessity for sympathetic, imaginative representation of the mind and experience" (*ibid.*, p. 288)—that is, for "introspection"—in addition to observation of the world without, a notion which Tuveson, I think improperly, associates with the Lockean principle of the dual source (sensation and "reflection") of our ideas (*ibid.*, p. 291). There is no indication in Tuveson's account of the vital function of the inward colloquy, as a method or process, in Shaftesbury's philosophy, despite a very refreshing recognition of Shaftesbury's interest in the psychopathological, the wicked, and the deformed or corrupt in human nature (*ibid.*, pp. 284–88) as well as the benevolent and beautiful. See the comment on Tuveson's article by A. D. McKillop in *Philological Quarterly*, XXXIII (1954), 296–97.

There are a number of useful studies of Shaftesbury's critical doctrines already available; see esp. A. O. Aldridge, "Shaftesbury and the Test of Truth," *PMLA*, LX (1945), 129–56 and "Lord Shaftesbury's Literary Theories," *Philological Quarterly*, XXIV (1945), 46–64; R. L. Brett, *The Third Earl of Shaftesbury: A Study in Eighteenth-Century Literary Theory* (London, 1951). The present discussion therefore concentrates largely on the special significance which the conceptions of self-knowledge and inward colloquy have in his treatment of the three themes of dialectical poetic theory.

3 Cecil A. Moore, *English Prose of the Eighteenth Century* (New York, 1933), pp. 357–58. See also Tuveson, *op. cit.*, pp. 277–78; W. Sypher, *Enlightened England* (New York, 1947), p. 63; M. Sherwood, *Undercurrents of Influence in English Romantic Poetry* (Cambridge, Mass., 1934), pp. 34–48, esp. pp. 39–43; E. Cassirer, *The Platonic Renaissance in England* (Austin, Tex., 1953), pp. 183–200, esp. pp. 186–87, 194–96.

impracticable without a previous commerce with the world";
yet given that necessary (but "non-instinctive") material on
which to work it is a very useful "art," and the larger one's
commerce with the world "the more practicable and improving" the method "is likely to prove."[4] It is thus especially
useful in the "reformation" of corrupted taste:

> Whatever philosopher, critic, or author is convinced of this
> prerogative of nature, will easily be persuaded to apply him-
> self to the great work of reforming his taste, which he will
> have reason to suspect, if he be not such a one as has deliber-
> ately endeavoured to frame it by the just standard of nature.
> Whether this be his case, he will easily discover by appealing
> to his memory; for custom and fashion are powerful seduc-
> ers; and he must of necessity have fought hard against these
> to have attained that justness of taste which is required in
> one who pretends to follow nature. But if no such conflict
> can be called to mind, 'tis a certain token that the party has
> his taste very little different from the vulgar. And on this
> account he should instantly betake himself to the wholesome
> practice recommended in this treatise. He should set afoot
> the powerfullest faculties of his mind, and assemble the best
> forces of his wit and judgment, in order to make a formal
> descent on the territories of the heart; resolving to decline
> no combat, nor hearken to any terms, till he had pierced into
> its inmost provinces and reached the seat of empire. No
> treaties should amuse him; no advantages lead him aside.
> All other speculations should be suspended, all other mys-
> teries resigned, till this necessary campaign was made and
> these inward conflicts learnt; by which he would be able to
> gain at least some tolerable insight into himself and knowl-
> edge of his own natural principles.[5]

The widespread conception of Shaftesbury as the systematic
originator of, or catalytic agent for, the tradition of natural

---

[4] "Misc. Refl." III. 1 (II, 252).
[5] *Solil*. III. 3 (I, 228–29).

intuitional benevolism in British ethical theory is inadequate and misleading; for the natural human benevolence which Shaftesbury espoused is a kind naturally subject to abortion, atrophy, and especially corruption, unless it is properly developed and regulated according to a higher order of things. Taken all together, his writings reveal an awareness of actual human weakness and "illness"—in the various forms of irrationality, selfishness, dullness, pettiness, dishonesty, and all the rest—which draws him closer, in general orientation, spirit, and literary motive, if not in specific doctrine, to the period's great moral satirists, Swift and Pope, neither of whom would normally be identified with the tradition of natural benevolism.[6]

Shaftesbury's works treat of a variety of topics, but always in relation to a fundamental opposition between the ultimate, better form of things manifest in the whole universe (as the source of real being and value) and the immediate, limited, partial state of things. Like Plato, the Stoics, and the various Christian Platonists with whom he was conversant, Shaftesbury is concerned with the problems of regulating human ac-

---

6 As Tuveson has pointed out, the notion of the actual and simple "natural goodness" of man so commonly associated with Shaftesbury is at best misleading, because it requires that we ignore his deep awareness of human weakness and disorder and his own overt attempts at social correction (*op. cit.*, pp. 274–76). Tuveson, however, seriously distorts Shaftesbury's ethical position, not only by failing to see the importance of the inward colloquy per se but also, more generally, by trying to bring Shaftesbury into line with Locke and the general tradition of non-dialectical naturalists in ethical theory (*ibid.*, pp. 277–79). According to Shaftesbury "the task of the human being" is not, as Tuveson puts it (*ibid.*, pp. 277–78), "to retain a natural and original moral sense, instead of to attain it by a long course of redemption," but rather, quite otherwise, to develop a potential moral sense, or to "reform" actually corrupt moral inclinations and habits, according to the divine standard embodied in nature, by a "long course" of self-examination and criticism which will in fact culminate in a kind of "redemption," but one in which the man himself is responsible for the actuality of his state of grace or harmony with the ultimate order of things.

tions, ideas, passions, and creations according to the supreme order of the larger whole of the universe, of which men are organic parts. The inward colloquy functions in this scheme as the principal means of developing and redeeming the better aspects of the human soul, which are in pre-established harmony with the ultimate order of things—somewhat as the Socratic conversation may function in Plato's scheme to "give birth" to the innate ideas which correspond to the eternal forms. The method is the key instrument of all true understanding, of all determinations of right feeling and action, and of all perceptions of real beauty. It is relevant, therefore, to all possible subjects and to all men in general, though Shaftesbury judges that "the case of authors in particular" is "the most urgent," for these are the "gentlemen, whom it so highly imports to know themselves, and understand the natural strength and powers as well as the weaknesses of a human mind."[7]

Undoubtedly, however, in this qualified sense he did believe in a natural principle of benevolence or a moral sense, a natural capacity to feel the truly just and morally beautiful, which, in good Stoic fashion, is essentially in harmony with the rational principles of the universe. It is this common sense, indeed, which makes the activity of moral and social satire meaningful at all. In *Sensus Communis; An Essay on the Freedom of Wit and Humour,* he works out the details of his argument concerning the value of "ridicule" for which he was so frequently attacked.[8] The argument has a double basis, as the title clearly suggests. In the first place, he asserts that the presence of the *sensus communis* in men enables moral truth to emerge from all acts of wit and raillery, for if a satire is falsely grounded or excessive, men will tend naturally to perceive it to be so. In the second place, wit and raillery must therefore be accorded absolute freedom. Any object or human act may

---

[7] *Solil.* I. 2 (I, 124).
[8] See Aldridge, *op. cit.,* pp. 129–56.

be satirized; if some are held to be inviolable and come to be too well protected by official dogma, they may not be accurately viewed, and may even be "killed" by want of exercise and self-defense.[9]

The weight of the argument is carried chiefly by the doctrine of common sense, and Shaftesbury makes an effort to support that doctrine by means of a dialectical analysis of historical and experiential evidence. Actual differences of attitude and expressed opinion concerning the moral nature of man do not confute the existence of the common natural affection.[10] That common affection may be corrupted, and this is precisely what has happened in the various historical instances of conflicts of opinion even among the philosophers. One form of the corruption is found in such unhumanistic, "selfish" writers as Lucretius and Hobbes. Yet even those who deny the existence of a natural predisposition in man toward outward love, friendship, and brotherhood—who translate such conceptions into the play of self-love and interest—betray the universal presence and influence of the natural common sense by their very acts of writing for us to read. This does not mean, of course, that there are no actually malevolent men or that all acts of writing are consciously intended to express love for mankind, but rather that the act of communicating ideas (whatever their special character) is an automatic manifestation and sign of the author's natural sense of common affection or benevolence—a sign of the real unity in diversity.[11]

---

[9] *Sensus Communis* II. 3 (I, 66). See also *A Letter Concerning Enthusiasm* II (I, 15), *The Moralists, A Philosophical Rhapsody* I. 3 (II, 22), and *Solil.* II. 2 (I, 150, 154–55), where Shaftesbury states the related doctrine that the universe is a complex unity in diversity and that, given true freedom, the natural benevolence and truth will tend to dominate in society.

[10] See "Philosophical Regimen," *The Life, Unpublished Letters, and Philosophical Regimen of Anthony, Earl of Shaftesbury,* ed. Benjamin Rand (London and New York, 1900), pp. 1–12; esp. pp. 8–9.

[11] *Sens. Com.* II. 2 (I, 63–64). See also *Moral.* III. 2 (II, 136–37): "If this, I told him, were as he represented it, there could never, I thought, be any disagreement among men concerning actions and behaviour, as which

Largely on this dialectical basis Shaftesbury can argue finally that "the very spirit of faction, for the greatest part, seems to be no other than the abuse or irregularity of that social love and common affection which is natural to mankind." [12]

The same general line of reasoning is employed in the related, and not entirely separable, context of literary and artistic "taste." Its importance for Shaftesbury's own objectives and practice as an author is suggested by his observation that "the goddess PERSUASION must have been in a manner the mother of poetry, rhetoric, music, and the other kindred arts" [13]—all those arts, that is, of "moving the affections"— since these arts can progress and develop, through exercise, only if persuasion rather than force is the main political instrument in society, and only if the public is in a position to develop freely its natural taste and thus to be led by men of ability and wisdom. At the same time, these men of ability and wisdom must be charged with the "promotion" of the public taste:

> If therefore it so happened in these free communities, made by consent and voluntary association, that after awhile the power of one or of a few grew prevalent over the rest; if force took place, and the affairs of the society were administered without their concurrence by the influence of awe and terror; it followed that these pathetic sciences and arts of speech were little cultivated since they were of little use. But where

was base, which worthy; which handsome, and which deformed. But now we found perpetual variance among mankind, whose differences were chiefly founded on this disagreement in opinion; 'the one affirming, the other denying that this, or that, was fit or decent.'
"Even by this, then, replied he, it appears there is fitness and decency in actions; since the fit and decent is in this controversy ever pre-supposed. And whilst men are at odds about the subjects, the thing itself is universally agreed." Cf. *An Inquiry Concerning Virtue or Merit* II. 4 (I, 256–58).

[12] *Sens. Com.* III. 2 (I, 77).
[13] *Solil.* II. 2 (I, 154).

persuasion was the chief means of guiding the society; where the people were to be convinced before they acted; there elocution became considerable, there orators and bards were heard, and the chief geniuses and sages of the nation betook themselves to the study of those arts by which the people were rendered more treatable in a way of reason and understanding, and more subject to be led by men of science and erudition. The more these artists courted the public, the more they instructed it. In such constitutions as these 'twas the interest of the wise and able that the community should be judges of ability and wisdom. The high esteem of ingenuity was what advanced the ingenious to the greatest honours. And they who rose by science and politeness in the higher arts could not fail to promote that taste and relish to which they owed their personal distinction and pre-eminence.[14]

He then distinguishes several manners or qualitative modes of writing (as distinct from literary forms and "manners of imitation") relevant to the general task of criticism which are variously appropriate to the peculiarities of different situations, subjects, and audiences. The methodic mode is not exalting, but it is powerful and commanding. It subdues the mind and strengthens its determinations. It forms maxims better than any other mode, but it is rhetorically ineffective in most societies. The sublime and enthusiastic mode is inappropriate, in general, to critical subjects; the sublime can be the subject of criticism but not the means. The simple mode is the purest imitation of nature; but it is practically useful only when the palate of the audience is already formed to a "taste of real simplicity." But the playful satiric mode is particularly useful in a quarrelsome and selfish but largely free society such as Shaftesbury conceived his own to be, and the "home-wits," he says, would perhaps meet with considerable success in developing and reforming the public taste if they

---

14 *Ibid.* (I, 154–55).

refined the old pattern of this mode as found in ancient comedy and satire.[15] The problem here is one of social persuasion, not simply of knowledge or understanding, and Shaftesbury obviously considered his own role as an author to be that of a social commentator and critic, in a society much in need of improvement and guidance, more than that of a professional, systematic philosopher. Those of his writings published during his life are largely a collection of loosely organized and "familiar" dialogues, conversational epistles, and "soliloquies," which bear closer resemblance to the Horatian mode of satire than to the literary modes of any essentially philosophical school or tradition.

The grounds of criticism and satire, however, are not, in Shaftesbury's system, determined finally by the accidents of social custom and fashion; his writings also tend to approximate concretely the critical, examining method of inward colloquy, upon the authority of which all acts of judgment must be based. It is a dialectical method, and Shaftesbury's writings, even at their most methodic, proceed discursively less by systematic syllogistic induction or deduction than by a process of relating, opposing, expanding, and purifying the meanings of key terms and ideas which is, as it were, an imitation of the basic process of self-examination he so strongly emphasizes. It is never possible to confine him to systematic and consistent use of single, univocal meanings of terms because the development of his arguments always depends upon the range of those possible meanings available in common life and thought that can be incorporated, related, and properly controlled in reflection, conversation, or debate. The dialectic of critical examination, whether in the form of the personal inward colloquy as such or in the more social forms of dialogues and satires, is the controlling means by which, in Shaftesbury's view, the widest range of common ideas and feelings may be examined,

---

15 *Ibid.* (I, 157–69).

defined, and given their proper status according to the true, natural order of things.

POETRY AND PHILOSOPHY

An analogy between social criticism or satire and the philosophic process of self-criticism informs the bulk of Shaftesbury's writings, and it is particularly significant in his discussion of the nature and value of poetry. In its immediate social purpose and status, the work of the poet falls under the general head of "persuasion"; it is an art of "moving the affections." But this is not an ultimate definition, and according to Shaftesbury the poet, whether comic, tragic, or epic, is in competition with the philosopher. All writers, indeed, are "copyists" after nature, whatever style or manner they may happen to employ; [16] it is therefore appropriate to look for the common criteria which may be established for poets and those philosophers (at least) who write down their speculations and exhortations. At the ordinary rhetorical level of considering what most audiences demand of any writer, one such criterion is found in the morality of the writer's subject matter. "So much the poet must necessarily borrow of the philosopher as to be master of the common topics of morality. He must at least be speciously honest, and in all appearance a friend to Virtue throughout his poem. The good and wise will abate him nothing in this kind; and the people, though corrupt, are in the main best satisfied with this conduct." [17]

At a higher, less "specious" level, all manners and styles of writing, as imitations of nature, may be calculated to achieve the common philosophical objectives of moral and intellectual improvement—of the author himself, of the audience, or of both—and the principal question here is that of the sort

---

[16] *Ibid.* III. 3 (I, 228).
[17] *Ibid.* II. 3 (I, 181).

of nature to be imitated. Characteristically, a distinction can be made between a superior and an inferior order of things.

> Every one is a virtuoso of a higher or lower degree. Every one pursues a Grace and courts a Venus of one kind or another. The *venustum*, the *honestum*, the *decorum* of things will force its way. They who refuse to give it scope in the nobler subjects of a rational and moral kind will find its prevalency elsewhere in an inferior order of things. They who overlook the main springs of action, and despise the thought of numbers and proportion in a life at large, will, in the mean particulars of it, be no less taken up and engaged, as either in the study of common arts, or in the care and culture of mere mechanic beauties. The models of houses, buildings, and their accompanying ornaments; the plans of gardens, and their compartments; the ordering of walks, plantations, avenues; and a thousand other symmetries, will succeed in the room of that happier and higher symmetry and order of a mind.[18]

Although the inclination toward order and symmetry is natural and universal, manifesting itself in numerous forms of human activity, those writers who are able to capture the higher qualities of *mind* far outshine those who are content merely to copy external appearances or to achieve "mechanic beauties" of verse and style. The poet's art of imitating human life is by its very nature a higher kind of art than any of those limited only to external scenes and objects. Yet even the poet must actively *strive* to reveal true beauty in portraying the higher symmetry and order of mind (as well as in achieving symmetry and order in the manifest structures of his poems). The true poet, as the man of "invention" and "design," seeks to avoid the irregularities and extreme particularities of the appearances of nature; he forms the idea of his work from many particulars in which he can perceive

---

18 *Sens. Com.* IV. 2 (I, 92). See also *Solil.* I. 3 (I, 135).

the universal qualities of order and proportion, not from any servile copying of minute and singular features. Moreover, unlike the mere historian who copies exactly what he sees, the true poet apprehends in the appearances of human nature the ideal principles and forms of beauty and moral truth. The poetry that results shares with history and oratory, in their better forms, the proper portrayal of universal human character, and with philosophy, in its better form, the expression of moral truth itself.[19]

The method of inward colloquy has its special significance in this connection chiefly as the preliminary corrective by which the objective of accurate, natural description, upon which all writing depends, can be achieved.[20]

> It must, beyond any other science, teach us the turns of humour and passion, the variety of manners, the justness of characters, and truth of things, which when we rightly understand we may naturally describe. And on this depends chiefly the skill and art of a good writer. So that if to write well be a just pretence to merit, 'tis plain that writers who are apt to set no small value on their art must confess there is something valuable in this self-examining practice and method of inward colloquy.[21]

But the "poetic" meaning of the method appears also in a more direct structural context, in relation to Shaftesbury's conception of the essential analogy between dramatic poems and philosophical dialogues.[22] The dialogue form of writing

---

[19] *Sens. Com.* IV. 3 (I, 96–97). See also "Misc. Refl." V. 2 (II, 330–32) and *Solil.* III. 3 (I, 214–17).

[20] *Solil.* I. 3 (I, 136–37n.).

[21] *Ibid.* III. 2 (I, 211).

[22] See *ibid.* II. 2 (I, 166n.). See E. R. Purpus, "The 'Plain, Easy, and Familiar Way': The Dialogue in English Literature, 1660–1725," *ELH,* XVII (1950), 47–58, for a general account, useful especially bibliographically, of the historical context of dialogue writing and theorizing about the genre, into which Shaftesbury's theory and practice may be placed.

portrays a kind of inward conversation in the sense that it involves two or more "selves" in active discussion or contention.[23] In all dialogues, moreover, characters of a higher order can be distinguished from those "second characters" of a lower sort; and these reflect both the fundamental distinction between ideal nature and the "ordinary pleasures and diversions of the fashionable world"[24] and the two basic aspects or parts of the soul. All human souls are essentially a duality in unity: "the chief principle of philosophy" is the "doctrine of two persons in one individual self," a doctrine which explains the soul's ability to be "both good and bad, passionate for virtue, and vice, desirous of contraries"[25] and suggests the real significance of the Delphic inscription "recognize yourself."[26] The history of poetry clearly reveals the importance of this principle of duality. The dialogue form, Shaftesbury argues, preceded both philosophy proper (the "profession" of philosophy) and dramatic imitation.

> The philosophical writings to which our poet [Horace] in his *Art of Poetry* refers, were in themselves a kind of poetry, like the mimes, or personated pieces of early times, before philosophy was in vogue, and when as yet dramatical imitation was scarce formed; or at least, in many parts, not brought to due perfection. They were pieces which, besides their force of style and hidden numbers, carried a sort of action and imitation, the same as the epic and dramatic kinds. They were either real dialogues, or recitals of such personated discourses; where the persons themselves had their characters preserved throughout, their manners, humours, and distinct turns of temper and understanding maintained, according to the most exact poetical truth. 'Twas not enough that these pieces treated fundamentally of

---

23 See *Solil.* I. 2 (I, 112–21); III. 1 (I, 182–84).
24 See "Preface," *Second Characters, or the Language of Forms,* ed. B. Rand (Cambridge, 1914), p. 3.
25 *Solil.* I. 2 (I, 121).
26 See *ibid.* (I, 113–23).

morals, and in consequence pointed out real characters and manners: they exhibited them alive, and set the countenances and complexions of men plainly in view. And by this means they not only taught us to know others, but, what was principal and of highest virtue in them, they taught us to know ourselves.[27]

They could do this principally because they acted as a kind of mirror of life, presenting the two fundamental characters within us.

In this, there were two faces which would naturally present themselves to our view: one of them, like the commanding genius, the leader and chief above-mentioned [i.e., as in the Socratic dialogues]; the other like that rude, undisciplined, and headstrong creature whom we ourselves in our natural capacity most exactly resembled. Whatever we were employed in, whatever we set about, if once we had acquired the habit of this mirror we should, by virtue of the double reflection, distinguish ourselves into two different parties. And in this dramatic method, the work of self-inspection would proceed with admirable success.[28]

It is therefore no wonder, Shaftesbury argues, that the poets were esteemed so highly in early times as "sages," for "it appears they were such well-practised dialogists, and accustomed to this improving method, before ever philosophy had adopted it." The good "dramatic" (or "personating") poet, "instead of giving himself those dictating and masterly airs of wisdom, makes hardly any figure at all, and is scarce discoverable in his poem. This is being truly a master." [29] Thus, reversing Plato's hierarchy of preferred poetic forms (in which the "dramatic" and the "mixed"—i.e., epic—forms are both inferior, philosophically, to the simple "narrative"), Shaftesbury eliminates

27 *Ibid.* I. 3 (I, 127–28).
28 *Ibid.* (I, 128–29).
29 *Ibid.* (I, 129–30).

the irony and designates as the highest form that which most closely resembles the philosophical dialogue. And the dialogue is the preferred form of philosophical writing because it most closely represents the "converse" of the two essential parts of the human soul; it is, as it were, a written inward colloquy. The poet's highest and most "improving" method will thus be a dramatic one analogous to the inward colloquy, for this is the method which most accurately mirrors the fundamental truth of human nature.

ENTHUSIASM AND GENIUS

The critical method of thought directly involved in the inward colloquy and imitated in dialogues and dramatic poems is essentially a rational method; it is in natural opposition to the "methods" of the external senses, the inordinate passions, partiality, prejudice, appetite, diseased and "persuasive" fancies,[30] and all else that may be called irrational. One of the tasks of Shaftesbury's *Letter Concerning Enthusiasm* is to examine the common idea of enthusiasm in relation to ancient conceptions of divine inspiration and demon-worship and to the fundamental distinction between the real and the unreal. The discussion begins with a simple opposition between "enthusiasm" and "reason"; here "enthusiasm," in its common meaning, denotes an irrational and melancholy possession of the mind, a condition which is justly condemned by reasonble and cheerful men. But it is typical of Shaftesbury's scheme that such a simple opposition can be resolved in terms of a better and a worse form of each of the opposed qualities.

He finds one principle of resolution in the example of ancient writers. In a manner resembling that of his treatment of the Epicureans and Hobbists who demonstrate their natural benevolence by writing down their "selfish" theories for

---

[30] See *ibid.* III. 2 (I, 199–211). See also "Philos. Reg.," *op. cit.*: "Fancies or Appearances," pp. 164–78; "Fancy and Judgment," pp. 207–8; "The Assents of Judgment," pp. 209–13.

all to read [31] he points to the telling fact that even "the cold [and rational] Lucretius makes use of inspiration, when he writes against it, and is forced to raise an apparition of Nature, in a divine form, to animate and conduct him in his very work of degrading Nature, and despoiling her of all her seeming wisdom and divinity." [32] Although, according to Shaftesbury, the Pythagoreans and Platonists may be called pro-enthusiasts, the Epicureans and Academics anti-enthusiasts, Epicurus himself left room for "visionary fancy." [33] And not only did ancient poets always have the habit of addressing the muses, but they consistently maintained the imagination of divine presence controlling or directing the production of poems.[34] There appears to be, as Epicurus saw, "a good stock of visionary spirit originally in human nature." [35] In ancient times it was possible for all men to enjoy the imagination of divine presence (if they wished) without the danger of evil consequences for society. But in modern times, largely because of the constrictions of the "authorities" in the various parts of life where "enthusiasm" might appear,[36] this natural spirit is limited mainly to love poetry, where it is largely harmless, and religion, where it tends to serve as justification for a variety of cruel, destructive, foolish, and generally immoral acts. In religion it becomes a sort of evil demon, or satanic force, through extravagance and misdirection; it operates, that is, under conditions in which the present welfare of man is consecrated to a future state, in which the natural basis of human society, general love and brotherhood, is violated—often by the official religious law of the land.[37]

Shaftesbury is not, however, rejecting all kinds or manners

---

[31] *Sens. Com.* II. 2 (I, 63–64).
[32] *Enthus.* VI (I, 36–37).
[33] *Ibid.* II (I, 14); V (I, 34–35).
[34] *Ibid.* I (I, 8); VI (I, 36).
[35] *Ibid.* (I, 35).
[36] *Ibid.* II (I, 14–16).
[37] *Ibid.* (I, 15).

of enthusiasm, even though he consistently speaks of it as an "imagination" or "feeling" rather than an actuality of divine presence. The undesirable condition which he describes is a corruption—a running astray—of a natural "spirit" which is not itself evil;[38] and he argues not only that the harmlessness of the enthusiastic spirit in ancient times was a result of the prevailing state of freedom in which it could be the object of wit and raillery,[39] but also that it is possible to distinguish between the feeling of divine presence which involves a deity conceived as good and just and that which involves a deity conceived as either indifferent or arbitrary. The latter may be called demon-inspiration, and even Lucretius did not call upon a demon. Ultimately, the argument suggests that many modern Christian enthusiasts are actually demonists, if not atheists, since, as Shaftesbury views it, the divinity of which they claim the presence lacks the attributes of goodness and wisdom which are essential to the true theist's[40] conception of God. The enthusiastic passion, however, is much the same in its various forms. When the feeling of divine presence is real (or "genuine"), it may be called "divine inspiration" to distinguish it from the false.

> For as some have well remarked, there have been enthusias-
> tical atheists. Nor can divine inspiration, by its outward
> marks, be easily distinguished from it. For inspiration is a
> real feeling of the Divine Presence, and enthusiasm [in most
> of its modern manifestations] a false one. But the passion
> they raise is much alike. For when the mind is taken up in
> vision, and fixes its view either on any real object, or mere
> spectre of divinity; when it sees, or thinks it sees, anything
> prodigious, and more than human; its horror, delight, con-
> fusion, fear, admiration, or whatever passion belongs to it,
> or is uppermost on this occasion, will have something vast,

---

38 See "Misc. Refl." II. 1 (II, 173–79); *Moral.* III. 2 (II, 129–30).
39 *Enthus.* II (I, 14–16).
40 See *Inq. Virtue* I. 1–2 (I, 239–42).

immane, and (as painters say) beyond life. And this is what gave occasion to the name of fanaticism, as it was used by the ancients in its original sense, for an apparition transporting the mind.[41]

It follows, in general, that, although poets as a class may very well be dependent upon some form of enthusiasm, the best poets will be those whose feeling of divine presence is genuine and can be associated with a true conception of divinity. It is largely in this way that the ancient respect for enthusiasm, for transporting rhapsodies, for the truly sublime, can most reasonably be retained and justified.

Something there will be of extravagance and fury, when the ideas or images received are too big for the narrow human vessel to contain. So that inspiration may be justly called divine enthusiasm; for the word itself signifies divine presence, and was made use of by the philosopher whom the earliest Christian Fathers called divine, to express whatever was sublime in human passions. This was the spirit he allotted to heroes, statesmen, poets, orators, musicians, and even philosophers themselves. Nor can we, of our own accord, forbear ascribing to a noble enthusiasm whatever is greatly performed by any of these. So that almost all of us know something of this principle.[42]

We must acknowledge, then, the universality of the principle of enthusiasm among men, but since, as usual, the problem for Shaftesbury is to distinguish the false from the true, the bad from the good, the question of enthusiasm, like all others, must be submitted to rational examination or criticism. To know enthusiasm as we should

---

[41] *Enthus.* VII (I, 37–38). "Immane": tremendous, huge, monstrous in size or strength (O.E.D.).

[42] *Ibid.* (I, 38–39). Shaftesbury's footnote on p. 38 presents instances from Plato (*Apology* 22B, *Phaedrus* 241E, *Meno* 99D) and Plutarch (*Cato Major* 22) in which the antiquity of the concept of enthusiasm as divine inspiration is shown, especially as a peculiarly Platonic principle.

and discern it in its several kinds, both in ourselves and others; this is the great work, and by this means alone we can hope to avoid delusion. For to judge the spirits whether they are of God, we must antecedently judge our own spirit, whether it be of reason and sound sense; whether it be fit to judge at all, by being sedate, cool, and impartial, free of every biassing passion, every giddy vapour, or melancholy fume. This is the first knowledge and previous judgment: "To understand ourselves, and know what spirit we are of." Afterwards we may judge the spirit in others, consider what their personal merit is, and prove the validity of their testimony by the solidity of their brain.[43]

In other words, the better kinds of enthusiasm will not be in opposition to reason, if they are not obviously in opposition to true divinity (and vice versa); and thus the notion of inspired poetry or inspired utterance of any kind may be meaningfully incorporated into a scheme of society that is both benevolent and rational.[44] Indeed, it is difficult to believe that any of our real enjoyments of the beauties in nature and art could subsist if there were no reference at least to some "higher majesty or grandeur. ... I know not, in reality, what we should do to find a seasoning to most of our pleasures in life, were it not for the taste or relish which is owing to this particular passion, and the conceit or imagination which supports it." [45]

With this kind of reasoning, Shaftesbury can justify a variety of presumably irrational phenomena, including the *je ne sais quoi* and the rapid, untutored natural genius.[46] And one might suppose that he would make a direct and meaningful connection, in relation to the production of poetry, between "genius" [47] and enthusiasm or divine inspiration,

---

43 *Enthus.* VII (I, 39).
44 See *Moral.* III. 1 (II, 99, 110); 2 (II, 129–30); and "Misc. Refl." II. 1–2 (II, 173–215).
45 "Misc. Refl." II. 1 (II, 175).
46 See *Solil.* III. 3 (I, 214); II. 2 (p. 151).
47 The term *genius* carries in Shaftesbury's philosophy the sometimes overlapping concepts of (1) a basically irrational demon or spirit (*ibid.* I. 2

through the ideas either of possession by a "daemon" (which was sometimes related etymologically, as well as semantically, to "genius") or of spontaneous generation (which is often made a characteristic of the inspired production of poetry). But he does not; for Shaftesbury, the true poetic genius is not ignorant of art or of the causes of art's effects and beauties, and in the sense of innate capacity genius is but a basic enabling condition, analogous to the other natural inner senses in men which must be developed and controlled.

> They who enter the public lists must come duly trained and exercised, like well-appointed cavaliers expert in arms, and well instructed in the use of their weapon and management of their steed. For to be well accoutred and well mounted is not sufficient. The horse alone can never make the horseman, nor limbs the wrestler or the dancer. No more can a genius alone make a poet, or good parts a writer in any considerable kind. The skill and grace of writing is founded, as our wise poet tells us, in knowledge and good sense.[48]

It is knowledge and good sense, moreover, of the highest sort. It is not merely "that knowledge which is to be learnt from common authors, or the general conversation of the world," but rather that which is to be learned "from those particular rules of art which philosophy alone exhibits."[49] Primitive poets were esteemed "sages" not because they were divinely inspired (though that they may have been) or because they were untaught "originals" (though that too they probably were), but because they were essentially philosophers; they had philosophical knowledge. Homer himself, the

---

[I, 112]), (2) natural ability in art (*ibid.* II. 2 [p. 151]), (3) peculiar character, nature, or power (*ibid.*, pp. 161–67; III. 1 [pp. 182–83]), and (4) high excellence in general (*ibid.* II. 2 [p. 159]). The common element among them is something like "power," and its is always possible, in Shaftesbury's dialectic, to view each in terms of a higher and lower form, especially in connection with the principle of the potential and the actual.
[48] *Ibid.* I. 3 (I, 127).
[49] *Ibid.*

"prince" and "patriarch" of poets,[50] is unexcelled as a por-
trayer of human life and manners; and in that regard he may
be called a great genius.[51] But, although Homer may have
"acquired" his imitative ability by way of continual divine
possession, it is not this higher enthusiasm as such which enti-
tles him to the name of "genius," and Shaftesbury's account
simply omits any reference to his lack of learning or to the
notion that, like Shakespeare, Homer was a child of nature
rather than an artist. It is enough for Shaftesbury, in short,
that Homer was a primitive "mimographer" [52]—an ingenious
imitator of men and manners who, with a masterly art like
that of Plato, allowed his characters to "show themselves."

> From hence possibly we may form a notion of that resem-
> blance which on so many occasions was heretofore remarked
> between the prince of poets and the divine philosopher who
> was said to rival him, and who, together with his contempo-
> raries of the same school, writ wholly in that manner of dia-
> logue above described. From hence too we may comprehend
> perhaps why the study of dialogue was heretofore thought
> so advantageous to writers, and why this manner of writing
> was judged so difficult, which at first sight, it must be owned,
> appears easiest of any.[53]

Poetic genius, then, in this higher sense, is more a matter

---

50 *Ibid.* II. 2 (I, 166).
51 "Genius," however, has reference in Shaftesbury's scheme to an expressive
and persuasive as well as an imitative or depictive activity. Although all
writing must be conceived as imitation of nature, it cannot be denied that
writers may express ideas as well as depict human nature, and even
Aristotle may be called a great genius (*ibid.* II. 2 [I, 159]). This is not
merely because genius may also mean "peculiar character" or "kind," but
because it may have reference, in general, to rhetorical power and command
of the expression of ideas. Socrates was a genius without being a writer
at all, and as the leading character of the philosophical dialogues he had
the role of expressing the ideal truth and persuading and criticizing the
"lower" characters (*ibid.* I. 3 [p. 128]).
52 *Ibid.* (I, 129).
53 *Ibid.* (I, 130).

of art and knowledge than of inspiration and rapture. There is no real conflict, however, between inspiration and art in Shaftesbury's scheme, precisely because the feeling of divine presence, like any other human feeling, may be purified and controlled, through the agency of the inward colloquy, according to those very principles of reason and good sense which entitle a poet to the name of artist.[54] Above all else, the poet must bring to his task a "moral genius" by which to achieve true proportion and beauty in his imitations of men and manners. And it is the method of inward colloquy which serves to help him "add the wisdom of the heart to the task and exercise of the brain" and thus to prepare him adequately for the achievement of the common objectives of philosophy and poetry.[55]

THE POET AS "SECOND MAKER"

The final justification, however, of Shaftesbury's conception of poetic art and genius must lie in the establishment of a positive relationship of some sort between the minds of men (at least of poets and philosophers) and the true order of things. The key to this relationship is suggested by his description of God as "sovereign genius" and "author" of the universe.[56] Shaftesbury makes full use of the principle of imitation of ancient writers, which is common in rhetorically oriented poetics, but he subordinates it to the principle of the imitation of divinity and the divine creative act; and it is mainly in this context that his view of the nature and value of poets and poetry is finally clarified and that his strong emphasis on the method of inward colloquy is given its final metaphysical significance.

He distinguishes two kinds of divine creativeness that are superior in power and value to human art. The first and high-

---

[54] See *ibid.* II. 3 (I, 171–80).
[55] *Ibid.* (I, 180–81).
[56] See *Moral.* III. 1 (II, 97–113).

est is that of the supreme creator himself, variously named
"sovereign genius," "divine author," "impowering deity," and
"sovereign mind." His "being" is "boundless, unsearchable,
impenetrable," but he is obviously benevolent, wise, and just,
as well as omnipotent. The second is Nature, which Shaftesbury calls an "impowered creatress" and "substitute of Providence." Her order is one of created beings, but she is also
herself a "creative power." [57] The sovereign genius apparently
created Nature, in his own image, to act as his "substitute"
and "representative." He is one, spiritual, and all-powerful;
Nature possesses these "active" attributes, but mixes them,
inevitably, with manifold, material, and passive ones, thus
tending to confuse our powers of explanation, and encourag-
ing us, as it were, to see inequity, disorder, and injustice in
the world. The active spirituality and unity in Nature remain
supreme, but it is her way to produce an infinite variety of
beings and modes of being, which, like Leibnizian monads,
nevertheless all reflect the spiritual unity of the supreme creator or sovereign genius. It is in this sense that different parts,
aspects, and creatures of Nature may be said to have different
"geniuses" and "selves," and also that Nature herself may be
said to be "divine." [58]

The special lines of relationship which Shaftesbury draws
between man and this divine, creative order of things involve,
first, an elaborate discussion of the source and foundation of
beauty. Although the universe of nature is a unified, beautiful
whole, its "external" beauties and enchantments are "only the

---

[57] *Ibid.* (II, 98). See also II. 4 (II, 79, 81) and III. 2 (pp. 132–33). Cf. "Philos.
Reg.," *op. cit.*: "Deity," pp. 13–39; "Providence," pp. 40–47; "Nature,"
pp. 184–88. One must be careful, in reading the works of Shaftesbury, to
avoid assigning single univocal meanings to key terms like *nature,* and at
this point especially it must be realized that he is quite capable of shifting from "nature" as a mixture of soul and body to "nature" as animating
soul or better form, from "nature" as the imperfect actual state of human
existence (cf. *Solil.* I. 3 [I, 128–29]) to "nature" as the just standard for controlling our basic instincts (*ibid.* III. 8 [pp. 228–29]).
[58] *Moral.* III. 1 (II, 101–2).

faint shadow of that first beauty" of the divine mind. The scenes of nature are nevertheless sought by lovers and poets, "and all those other students in nature and the arts which copy after her"—all who are "lovers either of the Muses or the Graces"—because they are "inspired" by the substance of the true beauty "represented" in natural scenes or because, more consciously, they admire the representative "for the sake of the original."[59] Even lovers and poets, then, do not find the object of their desire in body (or matter) itself, but in "forming power"—in the order and harmony which reflects the action and "art" of a mind.[60] This action of mind can be discerned in three "orders" of beauty available to man. First, "the dead forms . . . which bear a fashion, and are formed, whether by man or Nature, but have no forming power, no action, or intelligence." Second, "the forms which form, that is, which have intelligence, action and operation." Third, that "which forms not only such as we call mere forms but even the forms which form." The second order constitutes a kind of "double" beauty. "For here is both the form (the effect of mind) and mind itself. The first kind low and despicable in respect of this other, from whence the dead form receives its lustre and force of beauty. For what is mere body, though a human one, and ever so exactly fashioned, if inward form be wanting, and the mind be monstrous or imperfect, as in an idiot or savage?" The second order, however, is entirely dependent on the third. Although human beings have been given the habit of "producing" offspring like themselves, "this virtue of theirs" comes "from another form above them, and could not properly be called their virtue or art, if in reality there was a superior art or something artist-like, which guided their hand, and made tools of them in this specious work"; and although we human beings "are notable architects of matter, and can show lifeless bodies brought into form, and fash-

---

59 *Ibid.* III. 2 (II, 125–26).
60 *Ibid.* (II, 131–32).

ioned by our own hands . . . that which fashions even minds themselves, contains in itself all the beauties fashioned by those minds, and is consequently the principle, source, and fountain of all beauty." Therefore, "whatever beauty appears in our second order of forms, or whatever is derived or produced from thence, all this is eminently, principally, and originally in this last order of supreme and sovereign beauty." Whatever beauty may appear in "architecture, music, and all which is of human invention, resolves itself into this last order." [61]

The immediate relevance of all this consists in the fact that the human mind has the ability to apprehend and respond to all three forms of beauty, in their many peculiar manifestations. Like the lower animals, the human being possesses "instincts" or "pre-conceptions" through which Nature may be said to "teach," in a sense, "exclusive of art, culture, or discipline," [62] and men may experience thus a kind of direct inspiration, or "enthusiasm," from the various lower scenes of nature and art which may be "transferred" to the higher beauty—though of course not without considerable labor and pains.

> Are there senses by which all those other graces and perfections are perceived, and none by which this higher perfection and grace is comprehended? Is it so preposterous to bring that enthusiasm hither, and transfer it from those secondary and scanty objects to this original and comprehensive one? Observe how the case stands in all those other subjects of

---

[61] *Ibid.* (II, 132–33). Shaftesbury's *Second Characters* (see note 24, above) is a group of essays devoted to the lower order of forms. The subtitle, *The Language of Forms,* suggests that it is possible to perceive in them something beyond mere "dead" structure, namely, a kind of "communication." And it is Shaftesbury's hope that by "these SECOND CHARACTERS, or underparts, he can be able in the least degree to support those higher which he once sustained in behalf of the chief concerns and interests of mankind" (Preface, p. 3).

[62] *Moral.* III. 2 (II, 135).

art or science. What difficulty to be in any degree knowing! How long ere a true taste is gained! How many things shocking, how many offensive at first, which afterwards are known and acknowledged the highest beauties! For 'tis not instantly we acquire the sense by which these beauties are discoverable. Labour and pains are required, and time to cultivate a natural genius ever so apt or forward. But who is there once thinks of cultivating this soil, or of improving any sense or faculty which Nature may have given of this kind? And is it a wonder we should be dull then, as we are, confounded and at a loss in these affairs, blind as to this higher scene, these nobler representations? Which way should we come to understand better? Which way be knowing in these beauties? Is study, science, or learning necessary to understand all beauties else? And for the sovereign beauty, is there no skill or science required? In painting there are shades and masterly strokes which the vulgar understand not, but find fault with; in architecture there is the rustic; in music the chromatic kind, and skilful mixture of dissonancies: and is there nothing which answers to this in the whole? [63]

Man is not limited, however, to mere contemplation of the higher beauty, and he is not limited, in his own exertions of "forming power," to the production of the "dead" forms of art. There is a sense in which men may actually become forms which form minds, and thus resemble more closely the supreme creator himself. Human minds, as a fact of nature, are a duality of good and bad, or better and worse, and a man may assume the task of "forming" his own mind so as to develop— to give birth to—the better parts.[64] And thus Shaftesbury returns to the crucially important method of inward colloquy; by this method,

the improving mind, slightly surveying other objects, and passing over bodies and the common forms (where only a

---

63 *Ibid.* (II, 129–30).
64 *Ibid.* (II, 134).

shadow of beauty rests), ambitiously presses onward to its source, and views the original of form and order in that which is intelligent. And thus . . . may we improve and become artists in the kind; learning "to know ourselves, and what that is, which by improving, we may be sure to advance our worth and real self-interest." For neither is this knowledge acquired by contemplation of bodies, or the outward forms, the view of pageantries, the study of estates and honours; nor is he to be esteemed that self-improving artist who makes a fortune out of these, but he (he only) is the wise and able man, who with a slight regard to these things, applies himself to cultivate another soil, builds in a different matter from that of stone or marble; and having righter models in his eye, becomes in truth the architect of his own life and fortune, by laying within himself the lasting and sure foundations of order, peace, and concord.[65]

In this kind of exalted context Shaftesbury's conception of the poet as a "second maker," as an imitator of the supreme creator as well as of "nature," is made precise. Those artists "who design merely after bodies, and form the graces of this sort, can never, with all their accuracy or correctness of design, be able to reform themselves, or grow a jot more shapely in their persons." But the better poets are among those artists who "copy from another life, who study the graces and perfections of minds," and it is impossible that they "should fail of being themselves improved, and amended in their better part." [66] The true poet, in fact, is "a real master, or architect in the kind," who "can describe both men and manners, and give to an action its just body and proportions. . . . Such a poet is indeed a second *Maker; a just Prometheus under Jove*. Like that sovereign artist or universal plastic nature, he forms a whole, coherent and proportioned in itself with subjection and subordinacy of constituent parts," but, more than this, he

---

[65] *Ibid.* III. 3 (II, 144).
[66] *Solil.* I. 3 (I, 135).

knows "the boundaries of the passions" and "their exact tones and measures," and through this knowledge "represents them, marks the sublime of sentiments and action, and distinguishes the beautiful from the deformed, the amiable from the odious." The "moral artist who can thus imitate the Creator, and is thus knowing in the inward form and structure of his fellow-creature, will hardly . . . be found unknowing in himself, or at a loss in those numbers which make the harmony of a mind." [67] He will be, in short, a maker of *mind*—his own—as well as of poems which accurately and beautifully personate the forms and qualities of human nature. Like the creative "substitute of Providence," he thus partakes of divine creativity, and it is in this sense that he is most aptly and most significantly called an imitator of Nature.

Poetry is also, however, an art of "moving the affections" of others, and falls under the general head of "persuasion"; although Shaftesbury does not (and, given his conception of the perfectly self-sufficient creator, cannot) adopt the Platonic doctrine of the "persuasive" act of the divine creator in bringing recalcitrant materials into harmony and order, [68] the concept of persuasion appears, as an attribute or power of deity, in another sense. Through created things a contact between the mind of God and the mind of man is made; in Shaftesbury's view, it is characterized, in the recipient, both by intellectual apprehension and by *feeling*, by movements of the affections. A true poet, therefore, imitates the sovereign genius also in the act of causing his fellow human beings to think and to feel in a condition of harmony with the true principles of reality; he is especially God-like when he causes them to recognize themselves in the mirror of human nature which he

---

[67] *Ibid.* (I, 136).
[68] Plato *Timaeus* 48A: "Mind, the ruling power, persuaded necessity to bring the greater part of created things to perfection, and thus and after this manner in the beginning, when the influence of reason got the better of necessity, the universe was created" (Jowett).

presents for their benefit. Poets who imitate human geniuses like Homer and Plato are actually imitating poets who themselves imitated God both in the sense of being "second makers" of unified, harmonious, and justly proportioned moral wholes and in the sense of being, through their creations, wise, benevolent, and powerful regulators of the thoughts, affections, actions, and tastes of men. Thus the true poet may be said to be an important regulator of human society through a kind of persuasion and criticism which resembles the persuasion, in the form of Nature, by which the "author" of the universe regulates the whole of created being. For when men are inspired by Nature, or when they obey their inner senses (by which Nature rightly teaches), they experience, as it were, a divine persuasion or "enchantment" that can be nothing else but wise, benevolent, and just. And when poets bring to their innate abilities the powers of criticism and art (by which their poems rightly teach), they are able to regulate and improve not only themselves but also those who contemplate their creations and expressions.

But the practical significance of this argument finally rests on the critical method of inward colloquy. For this method itself commonly begins with a kind of inward rhetoric and persuasion, by which appearances are distinguished from reality, by which the false philosopher or poet may be distinguished from the true:

> And here it is that our sovereign remedy and gymnastic method of soliloquy takes its rise; when by a certain powerful figure of inward rhetoric the mind apostrophises its own fancies, raises them in their proper shapes and personages, and addresses them familiarly, without the least ceremony or respect. By this means it will soon happen that two formed parties will erect themselves within. For the imaginations or fancies being thus roundly treated are forced to declare themselves and take party. Those on the side of the elder

brother Appetite are strangely subtle and insinuating. They have always the faculty to speak by nods and winks. By this practice they conceal half their meaning, and, like modern politicians, pass for deeply wise, and adorn themselves with the finest pretexts and most specious glosses imaginable; till, being confronted with their fellows of a plainer language and expression, they are forced to quit their mysterious manner, and discover themselves mere sophisters and imposters who have not the least to do with the party of reason and good sense.

. . . He who deals in characters must of necessity know his own, or he will know nothing. And he who would give the world a profitable entertainment of this sort, should be sure to profit, first, by himself. For in this sense, Wisdom as well as Charity may be honestly said to begin at home. There is no way of estimating manners, or apprising the different humours, fancies, passions, and apprehensions of others, without first taking an inventory of the same kind of goods within ourselves, and surveying our domestic fund.[69]

The method of inward colloquy thus stands both as instrument and as symbol of the proper regulation of the inner springs of human life, and it is centrally relevant to poets and poetry because in Shaftesbury's dialectic, as in Plato's, the poet must strive to be a man of the highest philosophical and social usefulness, and worthy thus of the highest esteem, as well as a writer of poems. The inward colloquy is the principal means by which such nobler abilities are acquired, for it is through inner converse and debate that the poet struggles to acquire his perception of the ideal forms of human life.

---

[69] *Solil.* I. 2 (I, 123–24).

⫷ 3 ⫸

Akenside and the Powers of Imagination

ACCORDING TO THE "DESIGN" PREFIXED TO THE FIRST "version" of the poem (1744), Mark Akenside's *The Pleasures of Imagination* was written not only to "give a view" of the principles, operations, and pleasures of imagination "in the largest acceptation of the term," but also, and more importantly, to "enlarge and harmonize the imagination" by "exhibiting the most engaging prospects of nature," and thus "insensibly dispose the minds of men to a similar taste and habit of thinking in religion, morals, and civil life." To this end he was careful "to point out the benevolent intention of the author of nature in every principle of the human constitution" discussed in the poem and to "unite the moral excellencies of life in the same point of view with the mere external objects of good taste; thus recommending them in common to our natural propensity for admiring what is beautiful and lovely." [1]

---

[1] *The Poetical Works of Mark Akenside,* ed. Alexander Dyce (London: William Pickering, 1845), p. 83. All page references are to this edition. This discussion does not attempt to deal with the question of the changes which Akenside began making shortly after the first publication of the poem, and therefore little reference has been made to the unfinished later version (1757–70) entitled "The Pleasures of *the* Imagination." For a useful account of some of the differences between the two versions see Jeffrey Hart, "Akenside's Revision of *The Pleasures of Imagination*," *PMLA,* LXXIV (1959), 67–74. None of the differences indicates any departure from the dialectical character of the scheme which Akenside set forth in 1744, though there are a number of clear doctrinal changes. Unless otherwise

A discussion of the pleasures of imagination is a highly appropriate means of carrying out this special social task, because the powers of imagination "hold a middle place between the organs of bodily sense and the faculties of moral perception. . . . Like the external senses, they relate to matter and motion; and, at the same time, give the mind ideas analogous to those of moral approbation and dislike."[2] And the "influence of the imagination on the conduct of life, is one of the most important points in moral philosophy. It were easy by an induction of facts to prove that the imagination directs almost all the passions, and mixes with almost every circumstance of action or pleasure."[3] Nor was the decision to write a poem rather than a prose treatise or essay an arbitrary one. Akenside is convinced that the proper literary means of achieving his purpose is a heightened kind of poetic song; for not only is he concerned to "charm" his readers, but also the subject of the poem, properly understood, tends almost constantly to enthusiasm, rapture, and admiration.[4] The realm of the pleasures of imagination is a "fair poetic region";[5] and "Majestic Truth," the proper guide and guardian of the poetic powers of fancy and fiction, always accompanies "eternal Harmony," the "Goddess of the lyre."[6]

---

specified, Roman and Arabic numerals indicate book and lines of the 1744 version.

[2] Design, 85–86. Thus, for example, some men, "by the original frame of their minds, are more delighted with the vast and magnificent, others on the contrary with the elegant and gentle aspects of nature. And it is very remarkable, that the disposition of the moral powers is always similar to this of the imagination; that those who are most inclined to admire prodigious and sublime objects in the physical world are also most inclined to applaud examples of fortitude and heroic virtue in the moral. While those who are charmed rather with the delicacy and sweetness of colours, and forms, and sounds, never fail in like manner to yield the preference to the softer scenes of virtue and the sympathies of a domestic life" (Note to III, 18; pp. 147–48).

[3] Note to III. 18, p. 147.

[4] Design, p. 85.

[5] I. 51.

[6] I. 18–23.

Whether or not the rapture and the charms of "poetic" harmony are really necessary in such an endeavor, it seems certain that the task which Akenside set for himself does demand a "harmonizing" method of thought and discourse in which key ideas and terms may readily and swiftly shift, through more or less obvious analogies, from one realm of being to another. The final judgments of things will always be made in relation to a controlling distinction between a better and a worse state or form (between, for example, the lower "mere external objects of good taste" and the higher "moral excellencies"); but Akenside cannot be content to be governed by literal distinctions, such as those commonly made between "aesthetics" (or "art") and "morals" (or between the proper provinces of poetry and philosophy), for his basic program involves an ennobling unification or harmonizing of these supposedly dissonant realms.

Nevertheless, he first sets out, as he tells us, to distinguish the imagination from our other faculties and "to characterize those original forms or properties of being, about which it is conversant, and which are by nature adapted to it, as light is to the eyes, or truth to the understanding," and he argues that into Addison's "three general classes of greatness, novelty, and beauty . . . we may analyze every object, however complex, which, properly speaking, is delightful to the imagination." [7] He does not say, however, that Addison's three classes are completely satisfactory for the purposes of the present work; an object pleasing to the imagination

> may also include many other sources of pleasure; and its beauty, or novelty, or grandeur, will make a stronger impression by reason of this concurrence. Besides which, the imitative arts, especially poetry, owe much of their effect to

---

[7] I have discussed Akenside's intellectual relations with Addison (with special reference to these three "classes") in "Akenside and Addison: The Problem of Ideational Debt," *Modern Philology*, LIX (1961), 36–48.

a similar exhibition of properties quite foreign [literally speaking] to the imagination, insomuch that in every line of the most applauded poems, we meet with either ideas drawn from the external senses, or truths discovered to the understanding, or illustrations of contrivance and final causes, or, above all the rest, with circumstances proper to awaken and engage the passions. It was therefore necessary to enumerate and exemplify these different species of pleasure; especially that from the passions, which, as it is supreme in the noblest work of human genius [tragedy and epic], so being in some particulars not a little surprising, gave an opportunity to enliven the didactic turn of the poem, by introducing an allegory to account for the appearance.[8]

After the analysis of these pleasures, "which hold chiefly of admiration, or naturally warm and interest the mind," it was appropriate to consider "a pleasure of a very different nature, that which arises from ridicule   the foundation of the comic manner in all the arts." Following this it was necessary to illustrate "some particular pleasures, which arise either from the relations of different objects one to another, or from the nature of imitation itself. Of the first kind is that various and complicated resemblance existing between several parts of the material and immaterial worlds, which is the foundation of metaphor and wit." This "resemblance" between the world of matter (external, inanimate things) and the world of non-matter (mind) seems to depend "in a great measure" upon

the early association of our ideas, and as this habit of associating is the source of many pleasures and pains in life, and on that account bears a great share in the influence of poetry and the other arts, it is therefore mentioned here and its effects described. Then follows a general account of the production of these elegant arts, and of the secondary pleasure,

---

[8] *Design*, p. 84.

as it is called, arising from the resemblance of their imitations to the original appearances of nature.[9]

The poem then concludes "with some reflections on the general conduct of the powers of imagination, and on their natural and moral usefulness in life." [10] And in this last part of his work Akenside explains how the various pleasures which he discusses are to be brought together and "harmonized." The powers of imagination serve not merely an "adventitious" purpose of entertainment or delight in human life but also a fundamentally moral and "philosophical" purpose of helping to direct the various actions, passions, and delights of men.[11] But the imagination may also be deceptive (and in this context Akenside usually calls it the "fancy"); it may *mis*direct the lives of men "by heightening some objects beyond their real excellence and beauty, or by representing others in a more odious or terrible shape than they deserve." The imagination itself must be regulated, therefore, "by the standard of nature and the general good"—in harmony "with the moral order of things." [12]

The question of who among men is responsible for the proper regulation of the public imagination is thus a central one; Akenside's announcement that his poem is designed partly to "enlarge and harmonize the imagination, and by that means insensibly dispose the minds of men to a similar taste in religion, morals, and civil life" suggests that he is himself willing, at least temporarily, to assume the responsibility. In God's plan for the whole of human society the "active powers" of different men are deliberately "attuned" to different aspects

---

9 *Ibid.*, pp. 84–85.

10 *Ibid.*, p. 85.

11 Note to III. 18, pp. 147–48.

12 *Ibid.*, p. 147. On the different lexical meanings of *imagination* and *fancy* in Akenside's poem see A. O. Aldridge, "Akenside and Imagination," *Studies in Philology*, XLII (1945), 769–92.

of the universe; the "hand of Nature" has imprinted a different "bias" on different minds.[13] To some, for example,

> she taught the fabric of the sphere,
> The changeful moon, the circuit of the stars,
> The golden zones of heaven: to some she gave
> To weigh the moment of eternal things,
> Of time, and space, and fate's unbroken chain,
> And will's quick impulse: others by the hand
> She led o'er vales and mountains, to explore
> What healing virtue swells the tender veins
> Of herbs and flowers; or what the beams of morn
> Draw forth, distilling from the clifted rind
> In balmy tears.[14]

To others, however, a more exalted view was given; the sons of Fancy (as they may be called) were destined to "higher hopes," were wrought "within a finer mould" and "temper'd with a purer flame":

> To these the Sire Omnipotent unfolds
> The world's harmonious volume, there to read
> The transcript of Himself. On every part
> They trace the bright impressions of his hand:
> In earth or air, the meadow's purple stores,
> The moon's mild radiance, or the virgin's form
> Blooming with rosy smiles, they see portray'd
> That uncreated beauty, which delights
> The mind supreme. They also feel her charms,
> Enamour'd; they partake the eternal joy.[15]

Although all Nature's children, whatever their peculiar biases, are given a measure of the potential powers of true taste,[16] those few who are more richly endowed ("only few possess /

---

13 I. 79–85.
14 I. 86–96.
15 I. 96–108.
16 III. 536.

Patrician treasures or imperial states") [17] must be the leaders of "fair culture's kind, parental aid." [18] Akenside begins his main discussion by offering to guide his readers to a view of the "loveliest" aspects of Nature:

> O! attend
> Who'er thou art, whom these delights can touch
> Whose candid bosom the refining love
> Of Nature warms, O! listen to my song;
> And I will guide thee to her favourite walks,
> And teach thy solitude her voice to hear,
> And point her loveliest features to thy view.[19]

POETIC FANCY AND THE FORMS OF BEING

All the objects of nature and art which delight the imagination can be "referred" initially to the three quasi-Addisonian "orders":

> . . . whate'er of Nature's pregnant stores,
> Whate'er of mimic Art's reflected forms
> With love and admiration thus inflame
> The powers of Fancy, her delighted sons
> To three illustrious orders have referr'd;
> Three sister graces, whom the painter's hand,
> The poet's tongue, confesses; the sublime,
> The wonderful, the fair.[20]

And it is in part in terms of this classification of the "original forms or properties of being" that Akenside's task of developing the general public taste for the higher moral and religious excellencies must be accomplished, for "the sublime, the wonderful, the fair" are the principal affective qualities of a great many objects of "good taste" in nature and art—at least in

---

17 III. 576–77.
18 III. 538.
19 I. 132–38.
20 I. 139–46.

the common view of things.[21] The virtue of "mimic art" in general is its ability to reproduce the natural pleasures of imagination by portraying the various forms of being which produce these pleasures "originally." Among the mimic arts, however, poetry is especially valuable because it can portray "every species and mode of being." Since its medium is language, which consists of "signs universally established and understood," poetry not only can bring the appearances of external nature back to "remembrance" but also (when it has grown more correct and deliberate) extend its imitation "beyond the peculiar objects of the imaginative powers." Language is the special medium of thought and passion, and therefore poetry, more than painting, sculpture, or music, can transcend the phenomena of sense and "matter and motion" and rise to an apprehension and portrayal of non-sensible, non-material things. Nevertheless, poetry is a "mimic" art, and external nature is among its chief objects of description or imitation.[22]

One of Akenside's central problems in determining the poet's special power and function is thus to indicate how the pictures of the different aspects of external nature can be related to the higher non-material forms of being. This is an important issue, because, although Akenside seeks to "enlarge and harmonize the imagination" and to rise above the mere external objects of good taste, he has begun by adopting Addison's principle that the "secondary" pleasures of the imagination proceed from "remembrance" of the natural material objects which produce the "primary" pleasures. The solution which he provides entails a rather complicated dialectical ar-

---

[21] Like Shaftesbury, Akenside defines the "taste" which he hopes to control and harmonize as an innate "inclination" which must be properly developed or "nurtured" (III. 515–42). At the same time, it is natural for differences of inclination to exist among men (see III. 546–50), and these peculiarities must be taken seriously by the poet who hopes to have an important effect on the tastes of men. See above, note 2.

[22] *Design*, pp. 83–84.

gument, not all of which is completely clear; its main lines, however, can be marked out.

Although he gives special emphasis at first to the lower Addisonian classification of the natural objects of human taste and imagination (sublimity, novelty, and beauty), Akenside proceeds immediately to draw connections between these three "graces" (and the pleasures which they help to explain) and the familiar triad of eternal ideas—the Good, the True, and the Beautiful. Sublimity and novelty are related to the Good and the True principally on the basis of "final causes"— that is, of God's reasons for implanting in men the inclination to delight in the great and the wonderful. Man was "so eminently rais'd / Amid the vast creation" to delight in "thoughts beyond the limit of his frame" (the sublime) so he would be encouraged

> to run
> The great career of justice; to exalt
> His generous aim to all diviner deeds;
> To chase each partial purpose from his breast;
> And through the mists of passion and of sense,
> And through the tossing tide of chance and pain,
> To hold his course unfaltering, while the voice
> Of truth and virtue, up the steep ascent
> Of nature, calls him to his high reward,
> The applauding smile of Heaven.[23]

The "bounteous providence of Heaven" also implanted in man's breast the desire

> Of objects new and strange, to urge us on
> With unremitted labour to pursue
> Those sacred stores that wait the ripening soul,
> In Truth's exhaustless bosom.[24]

---

[23] I. 151–66.

[24] I. 239–44. Akenside first distinguishes between the "new" and the "strange" or "wonderful," and then brings them together again; see Note to I. 240,

Beauty, however, the "Brightest progeny of Heaven,"[25] occupies a special position of honor and importance; she is, indeed, the supreme object of the imagination, for she is presented both as one of the quasi-Addisonian "graces" and as one of the higher eternal ideas. Although it is difficult to know how deliberately planned it was, this double character of beauty may be viewed as a convenient rhetorical aid in effecting the transition from the mere external objects of good taste ("beauty") to the higher moral and religious excellencies of life (Beauty). For when Akenside comes to "trace" the features of the quasi-Addisonian order he quickly departs from the common human perceptions and actions and their final causes (the Addisonian conceptions of general beauty and of excellence within the species designed to promote love between the sexes, which are really only the appearances of the higher form of Beauty)[26] and moves to a higher, more exalted level. In effect, then, the final cause of "beauty" is the eternal form of Beauty; at the same time, the eternal form of Beauty is presented as an instrument for the achievement and glorification of Truth and Virtue. Moreover, not only was Beauty sent to earth to be "the lovely ministress of Truth and Good / In this dark world," but "Truth and Good are one, / And Beauty dwells in them, and they in her, / With like participation."[27] Why, then, Akenside asks, do the "sons of earth"—as

---

pp. 141–42: "These two ideas are oft confounded; though it is evident the mere novelty of an object makes it agreeable, even where the mind is not affected with the least degree of wonder: whereas wonder indeed always implies novelty, being never excited by common or well-known appearances. But the pleasure in both cases is explicable from the same final cause, the acquisition of knowledge and enlargement of our views of nature: on this account, it is natural to treat of them together."

25 I. 280.

26 I. 283–340.

27 I. 372–76. The heavy emphasis in the poem on beauty may be viewed as a kind of foreshadowing of some of the doctrinal changes discernible in the second version, where "novelty" is not included as one of the primary bases of "imaginative" pleasure, and sublimity is incorporated, as it were,

distinct from those chosen minds "temper'd with a purer
flame"—attempt to separate her from the other eternal forms?
It is folly to try:

> Oh wherefore, with a rash, impetuous aim,
> Seek ye those flowery joys with which the hand
> Of lavish Fancy paints each flattering scene
> Where Beauty seems to dwell, nor once inquire
> Where is the sanction of eternal Truth,
> Or where the seal of undeceitful Good,
> To save your search from folly! Wanting these,
> Lo! Beauty withers in your void embrace,
> And with the glittering of an idiot's toy
> Did Fancy mock your vows.[28]

Beauty resides, in her consummate form, at the summit of
Akenside's "steep ascent"; and there it is that the coalescence
with Truth and Virtue is most complete and perfect. He seems
to combine here two modes of dialectical distinction: the
"real" versus the "apparent" and the "more" versus the "less."
Thus, the beauty of external visual nature, or of the human

---

fairly explicitly in the higher—the "infinite and all-comprehending"—form
of Beauty (see *The Pleasures of the Imagination*, Book I [1757], "Argument" and lines 547–65, 620–49). The "comprehensive" character of beauty
appears, however, almost as clearly in the first version; see I. 275–80, where
beauty is said to beam "on the enchanted heart/Love, and harmonious wonder, and delight/Poetic." And it should be remembered that the final
causes of both sublimity and novelty (virtue and truth) coalesce with
Beauty at the highest level of being, both sublimity and novelty functioning as the hand-maidens, so to speak, of Beauty, and Beauty, at the same
time, functioning as the ministress of truth and virtue. It is not a fact,
moreover, that Akenside abandoned "novelty" altogether in the second
version; see the "General Argument" of the second version (*Poetical Works*,
p. 153): "With the above-mentioned causes of pleasure, which are universal
in the course of human life, and appertain to our higher faculties, many
others do generally occur, more limited in their operation, or of an inferior origin: such are the novelty of objects, the association of ideas,
affections of the bodily senses, influences of education, national habits,
and the like."

[28] I. 378–87.

countenance when it shows no truth or goodness, may be called but the "appearance" of Beauty, and yet (because it is the product of divine goodness and power) the scale (or "mountain") of being as a whole is a "fair-proportion'd scale," and the "charms" of Beauty are diffused, as it were, in varying degrees, "Like rays effulging from the parent sun," throughout "the unbounded symmetry of things."[29] There are six main progressively "rising" levels of the scale of being, on each of which some degree of real Beauty may be said to "dwell": (1) "the effusive warmth / Of colours mingling with a random blaze"; (2) "variations of determin'd shape, / Where Truth's eternal measures mark the bound / Of circle, cube, or sphere"; (3) the unification (in "natural concretes") of "this varied symmetry of parts / With colour's bland allurement"; (4) "the blooming forms [plants] / Through which the breath of Nature has infus'd / Her genial power to draw with pregnant veins / Nutritious moisture from the bounteous earth, / In fruit and seed prolific"; (5) "Nature's charm, where to the full consent / Of complicated members [shapes], to the bloom / Of colour, and the vital change of growth, / Life's holy flame and piercing sense are given / And active motion speaks the temper'd soul [animal life]"; (6) the expression of "mind"—human and divine.[30]

Akenside strongly emphasizes the inferiority of mere inani-

---

[29] I. 478–80.

[30] I. 442–75. See the "Argument" of Book I; p. 86. Two overlapping dialectical distinctions are involved in this hierarchical scale, both entailing a distinction between "mind" and "non-mind." The first is between the lowest level and all the levels above; the blaze of colors, as Akenside presents it, lacks "determined shape" and is an object of sense rather than intellect, but the five higher levels all involve objects of intellect. The second distinction is between the fifth and sixth levels (active morality and mind) on the one hand and all the lower levels (including, perhaps, "dead" matter itself, as distinct from our perception of it) on the other. Unfortunately, Akenside does not provide enough clarification to enable us to determine what exact relations, if any, he intended to draw between these two distinctions.

mate or passive "external scenes," because they lack the affecting qualities of virtue and love (animals) or of genius and
design (the "expression" of "mind"). An important distinction
is made between animal life and all other forms of created
being; beauty is more conspicuous when "faithful dogs with
eagers airs of joy / Salute their fellows" than when "the stately
tree which Autumn bends / With blushing treasures" obeys
the "genial power" of "the breath of Nature." [31] The suggestion—although there is some ambiguity here—is that the moral
actions of animals as well as the artistic expressions and designs
of men should be referred to "mind." It is clear at least that
Beauty dwells

> There most conspicuous, even in outward shape,
> Where dawns the high expression of a mind . . . .
> Mind, mind alone, (bear witness earth and heaven!)
> The living fountains in itself contains
> Of beauteous and sublime: [32] here hand in hand,
> Sit paramount the Graces; here enthron'd,
> Celestial Venus, with divinest airs,
> Invites the soul to never fading joy.[33]

"Lifeless" and passive things thus do not cause the human
heart to stir, Akenside argues, with anything approaching its
response to the power of moral action and expressive mind.

> For what are all
> The forms which brute, unconscious matter wears,

---

[31] I. 457–73.

[32] Akenside's mentioning here only "the beauteous and the sublime" is a
general indication of his rather ambiguous treatment of novelty in the
first version of the poem. Cf. I. 537–50, where the God-given impulse to
seek truth or knowledge (the final cause of the pleasure of novelty) is
separated from the gift of "bright Imagination's rays," and III. 546–50,
where he makes but a twofold distinction in natural inclinations between
those who seek "The vast alone, the wonderful, the wild" and those who
seek "harmony, and grace / And gentlest beauty"; cf. also Note to III. 18,
pp. 147–48.

[33] I. 473–86.

Greatness of bulk, or symmetry of parts?
Not reaching to the heart, soon feeble grows
The superficial impulse; dull their charms,
And satiate soon, and pall the languid eye.
Not so the moral species, nor the powers
Of genius and design; the ambitious mind
There sees herself: by these congenial forms
Touch'd and awaken'd, with intenser act
She bends each nerve, and meditates well pleas'd
Her features in the mirror. For of all
The inhabitants of earth, to man alone
Creative Wisdom gave to lift his eye
To Truth's eternal measures; thence to frame
The sacred laws of action and of will,
Discerning justice from unequal deeds,
And temperance from folly.[34]

It follows that the poet who would charm his readers with
the higher forms of being should seek to describe those scenes
of nature which are expressive of mind and avoid the merely
passive and non-expressive. This does not mean, however, that
a literal restriction must be placed on the poet's proper subject matter. Indeed, his task is to accommodate his perception
of the higher reality to the actual tastes and habits of men;
and the powers of imagination—designed by the "benignant
Sire" to lead us more directly and "brightly" to love and admiration of the higher order of things—dress "in ten thousand
hues" the naked Virtue that rises "from the awful depth / Of
Truth's mysterious bosom," so that it "Assumes a various feature, to attract, / With charms responsive to each gazer's eye,
/ The hearts of men." [35] The significance of this is intensified
by the fact that human beings—strangely, it seems at first to
Akenside—do enjoy the higher kind of pleasure from scenes of
external, inanimate, originally non-expressive nature, both in

---

34 I. 526–43.
35 I. 545–54.

imitations and in the natural things. Why the "various aspects of the mind"[36] may produce the higher pleasure is clear
enough, but how does it happen that "various aspects" of lifeless matter may also produce it? This would appear to be
impossible, at least if the distinction between mind and non-
mind is to be taken seriously.

It is in part to solve this problem that Akenside turns to
the concept of "association." He does not adopt the Platonic
principle of "recollection" of the divine forms in the apprehension of their material embodiments, but he does provide
a doctrine of association resembling that which Plato used to
illustrate his principle of recollection.[37] In the active form of
Beauty, for example, the "ambitious mind" is able to recognize the expressive "semblance" of himself existing there.[38]
But the lower inanimate forms or levels of beauty (though
they may evoke a lower, "adventitious" kind of pleasure) are
inexpressive, however true it may be that they necessarily reflect the creative power of the divine mind. The problem,
therefore, is to establish a positive connection—or, as Akenside
put it, to learn "that secret harmony"—between the actual expression of mind and scenes of inexpressive matter:

> Some heavenly genius, whose unclouded thoughts
> Attain that secret harmony which blends
> The etherial spirit with its mould of clay;
> O! teach me to reveal the grateful charm
> That searchless Nature o'er the sense of man
> Diffuses, to behold, in lifeless things,
> The inexpressive semblance of himself,

---

36 III. 278.

37 *Phaedo* 73D: ". . . what is the feeling of lovers when they recognize a
lyre, or a garment, or anything else which the beloved has been in the
habit of using? Do not they, from knowing the lyre, form in the mind's
eye an image of the youth to whom the lyre belongs? And this is recollection" (Jowett).

38 I. 534.

Of thought and passion. . . .
            Whence is this effect,
This kindred power of such discordant things?
Or flows their semblance from that mystic tone
To which the new-born mind's harmonious powers
At first were strung? Or rather from the links
Which artful custom twines around her frame? [39]

The answer follows seemingly without hesitation, and the first alternative (that the secret harmony may be implanted at the mind's birth), although not explicitly rejected, is not explored. Man apparently beholds in lifeless things the inexpressive semblance of himself chiefly because of past associations of such things with others essentially expressive.

For when the different images of things,
By chance combin'd, have struck the attentive soul
With deeper impulse, or connected long,
Have drawn her frequent eye; howe'er distinct
The external scenes, yet oft the ideas gain
From that conjunction an eternal tie,
And sympathy unbroken. Let the mind
Recall one partner of the various league,
Immediate, lo! the firm confederates rise,
And each his former station straight resumes:
One movement governs the consenting throng,
And all at once with rosy pleasure shine,
Or all are sadden'd with the glooms of care. . . .
Such is the secret union, when we feel
A song, a flower, a name, at once restore
Those long connected scenes where first they mov'd
The attention: backward thro' her mazy walks
Guiding the wanton fancy to her scope,
To temples, courts or fields; with all the band
Of painted forms, of passions and designs
Attendant: whence, if pleasing in itself,

---

[39] III. 279–311.

The prospect from that sweet accession gains
Redoubled influence o'er the listening mind.[40]

In this way, the highest and most affecting object of the imagination—the *expression* of mind—can be said to pervade the
whole universe, even the inanimate forms of being: the inanimate forms may acquire intellectual or emotive associations
and through them be said to participate in the divine expressive forms. The mental "attributes" of matter derive, of
course, from the original powers of imagination. Men are
endowed by the deity with certain inclinations, not toward
different material things *as* material things but to different
kinds of intellectual and emotive values which may be attached, by association, to material things; mind itself is the
source of the "beauteous and sublime." [41] "Association" thus
helps to establish a practical continuum between the two principal levels of the "steep ascent." It defeats, as it were, an
impassible gap—at least in relation to the pleasures of imagination—between the realms of mind and matter, and does so
without requiring a denial of the original non-spiritual character of the material things or a contradiction of the fundamental principle of the inferiority of mere lifeless matter in
the scale of being. To argue, moreover, that man is formed
at birth to perceive adequately an analogy between the material and the immaterial would perhaps undermine somewhat
the very purpose for which Akenside is writing his poem—to
"*dispose* the minds of men" toward an enlarged and harmonized view of things.

---

40 III. 312–47. In the Design, p. 85, Akenside states that early "association of
ideas" is "in great measure" responsible for our perception of resemblance
between the material and the immaterial worlds, which is the foundation
of metaphor and wit. In the note to III. 285, he states that this resemblance
is the basis of "almost all the ornaments of poetic diction." Then in the
note to III. 348 he argues that the "act of remembering seems almost
wholly to depend on the association of ideas."
41 I. 481–83.

Akenside's conception of the function of association is therefore especially important in his theory of the art and affective power of poetry—particularly when the question concerns poetry in which images of external nature are essential or appropriate. It is largely by association that the "power" of Memory collects "all / The various forms of being to present, / Before the curious aim of mimic art, / Their largest choice." [42] And it is by virtue of what may be called universal or common associations—especially, as Akenside suggests,[43] in metaphor and "wit"—that the true poet can not only touch the collective springs of his readers' lower and merely "adventitious" inclinations and delights (such as those of external sensation and of self-interest, or of the "mere external objects of good taste") but also of their natural inclinations to love and admire the higher intellectual forms of God's true order of things.

The poet's ability, however, to infuse his pictures of the ordinary world with the higher charms of "immaterial" reality extends considerably beyond the description or imitation of external nature. The poet is characteristically concerned, for example, with depicting and evoking human passions; although the pleasures of the passions may be called "adventitious" (as specifically different from, though not opposed to, the pleasures of imagination as such), at the same time the passions are "directed" by the powers of imagination, and therefore potentially they may be controlled by perception of the higher forms of reality. When not misdirected, the feeling heart, Akenside says, is "above" the conventions and opinions of time or place; [44] human passion then is universal and real:

> Then Nature speaks
> Her genuine language, and the words of men,

---

42 III. 348–55.
43 Design, p. 85.
44 II. 136–49.

Big with the very motion of their souls,
Declare with what accumulated force,
The impetuous nerve of passion urges on
The native weight and energy of things.[45]

The application of this doctrine is not limited to the originally "pleasurable" or "admirable" passions; every human passion —pleasant or painful—may "to man / Administer delight" [46] and be representative of the true nature of things. Thus pleasure may flow from scenes of great pain; and it is this "very mysterious kind of pleasure" that is the "origin and basis of tragedy and epic." Lucretius falsely resolves it into self-love; the Abbé du Bos "accounts for it by the general delight which the mind takes in its own activity, and the abhorrence it feels of an indolent and inattentive state: and this, joined with the moral approbation of its own temper, which attends these emotions when natural and just, is certainly the true foundation of the pleasure." [47] The common pains of men actually serve benevolent and beautiful ends in God's true order. From the merely human point of view, the painful passions may appear to be opposed to both pleasure and true justice; from a more exalted point of view one can see them as productive of a nobler pleasure—if one can but remove from himself the fetters of partial and selfish conceptions of the universe.[48] And, again, it is the fact that the imagination is naturally conversant with the eternal forms, especially Beauty, which makes this higher pleasure possible.[49]

The general principle applies also to the satirist or comic poet, especially in his role as commentator on vice and folly. Human vice has its origins in the false representations of the imagination (or fancy), which produce "false opinions con-

---

45 II. 149–54.
46 II. 166–67.
47 Note to II. 157, pp. 144–45.
48 II. 669–771.
49 Note to III. 593, p. 152.

cerning good and evil." [50] And yet not all the "lying forms which Fancy in the brain / Engenders" automatically produce "guilty deeds" and bind "Reason . . . in chains, / That Vice alone may lord it." [51] On the contrary, often, like a queen, Folly may be said to mount the throne and play her "idiot antics" to make actually benevolent rebukes, and it is in this possibility that the true value of ridicule and the comic muse is found. The practice is of real social importance because the incongruity of Fancy's false pictures is always caught by the perceptive observer:

> Where'er the power of Ridicule displays
> Her quaint ey'd visage, some incongruous form,
> Some stubborn dissonance of things combin'd
> Strikes on the quick observer: whether Pomp,
> Or Praise, or Beauty, mix their partial claim
> Where sordid fashions, where ignoble deeds,
> Where foul Deformity, are wont to dwell,
> Or whether these with violation loath'd,
> Invade resplendent Pomp's imperious mien,
> The charms of Beauty or the boast of Praise.[52]

The practical "philosophic" value of ridicule is thus based on a natural sense much like Shaftesbury's *sensus communis;* "it is beyond all contradiction evident," Akenside says, "that we have a natural sense or feeling of the ridiculous." [53] It is bestowed upon us in order "to aid / The tardy steps of Reason, and at once / By this prompt impulse urge us to depress / The giddy aims of Folly." [54] Hence "one cannot, without astonishment, reflect on the conduct of those men who imagine it is for the service of true religion to vilify and blacken it without distinction, and endeavour to persuade us that it is

50 Argument of Book III, p. 123.
51 III. 62–66.
52 III. 249–58.
53 Note to III. 259, p. 150.
54 III. 262–65.

never applied but in a bad cause." [55] Its value, however, does not lie in the conduct of theoretical speculation, but in the practical evaluation of men and things; nevertheless it claims the power of truth.

> Ridicule is not concerned with mere speculative truth or falsehood. It is not in abstract propositions or theorems, but in actions and passions, good and evil, beauty and deformity, that we find materials for it; and all these terms are relative, implying approbation or blame. To ask then whether ridicule be a test of truth, is, in other words, to ask whether that which is ridiculous can be morally true, can be just and becoming; or whether that which is just and becoming, can be ridiculous. A question that does not deserve a serious answer. For it is most evident, that, as in a metaphysical proposition offered to the understanding for its assent, the faculty of reason examines the terms of the proposition, and finding one idea, which was supposed equal to another, to be in fact unequal, of consequence rejects the proposition as a falsehood; so, in objects offered to the mind for its esteem or applause, the faculty of ridicule, finding an incongruity in the claim, urges the mind to reject it with laughter and contempt. When, therefore, we observe such a claim obtruded upon mankind, and the inconsistent circumstances carefully concealed from the eye of the public, it is our business, if the matter be of importance to society, to drag out those latent circumstances, and, by setting them in full view, to convince the world how ridiculous the claim is: and thus a double advantage is gained; for we both detect the moral falsehood sooner than in the way of speculative enquiry, and impress the minds of men with a stronger sense of the vanity and error of its authors. And this and no more is meant by the application of ridicule.[56]

If someone argues that the practice is dangerous, that it "may be inconsistent with the regard we owe to objects of real

---

[55] Note to III. 259, p. 150.
[56] *Ibid.*, pp. 150–51.

dignity and excellence," the proper answer is that "the practice fairly managed can never be dangerous; men may be dishonest in obtruding circumstances foreign to the object, and we may be inadvertent in allowing those circumstances to impose upon us: but the sense of ridicule always judges right." [57] It is a "natural sense," given by God, which, like reason itself, may indeed be misused; but even in its misuse it is the natural faculty and still operates according to its proper natural laws.

> The Socrates of Aristophanes is as truly ridiculous a character as ever was drawn:——true; but it is not the character of Socrates, the divine moralist and father of ancient wisdom. What then? did the ridicule of the poet hinder the philosopher from detecting and disclaiming those foreign circumstances which he had falsely introduced into his character, and thus rendered the satirist doubly ridiculous in his turn? No; but it nevertheless had an ill influence on the minds of the people. And so has the reasoning of Spinoza made many atheists: he has founded it indeed on suppositions utterly false; but allow him these, and his conclusions are unavoidably true. And if we must reject the use of ridicule, because, by the imposition of false circumstances, things may be made to seem ridiculous, which are not so in themselves; why we ought not in the same manner to reject the use of reason, because, by proceeding on false principles, conclusions will appear true which are impossible in nature, let the vehement and obstinate declaimers against ridicule determine.[58]

The "comic muse" of ridicule, then, is no more inherently dangerous or despicable than the painful passions of tragedy or the sensory and ordinary imaginative pleasures of external nature—even though ridicule proceeds deliberately by means of the false appearances of Fancy. These products of Fancy

---

[57] *Ibid.*, p. 151.
[58] *Ibid.*

may be put to proper use in the true order of things; and God has designed it to be so, giving human beings a natural sense of ridicule, as he has given them a natural sense of tenderness and admiration by which the terrors and pains of human life may be transcended. If the application of ridicule is to be justified in ultimate terms, it must, like anything else, be controlled by the true forms of reality, and the fact that it may be misapplied in no way destroys its great social and philosophic value.

Thus does Akenside proceed to "unite the moral excellencies of life in the same point of view" with the "mere external objects of good taste"; the common "Addisonian" qualities of nature and the major forms of poetic art are brought into meaningful relation with the higher forms of being. And poetry is given an especially important function in the ultimate order of things not only in the general sense that the poet can apprehend and portray the higher forms of being to properly direct the thoughts, tastes, and feelings of men, but also in the special sense that some of the products of imagination or fancy may be very useful in the task of exposing human folly and vice.

GENIUS AND THE INSPIRATION OF BEAUTY

The various subjects which Akenside himself discusses in the poem all tend to reflect the special "expressive" and affective powers which he attributes to poetry in its various conventional forms and styles, and he tells us that he endeavored to produce the different characteristics of action, mood, imagery, and style that are appropriate to the poem's different topics. Thus, for example, when he discusses the human passions, and especially the painful ones, it seems appropriate to him to depart from the common "didactic" style and to employ an "allegory" in which a heroic character named Harmodius movingly and eloquently tells of his painful reaction to the evils of human life; of his futile railing against the great injustice of it all; and of his being brought at last to see the larger justice and beauty of God's order.[59] From this exalted "epic" subject, Akenside moves to his account of ridicule; and here too "a change of style became necessary," though one that would "be consistent, if possible, with the general taste of composition in the serious parts of the subject." [60] And in the passages describing those things especially ridiculous in human life he uses images, for example, of magical appearances of "tribes" or "motley bands" of "genii" and "forms" representing the various laughable vices and incongruities.[61] He declares that he had two principal models in producing this variety of styles: "that ancient and simple one of the first Grecian poets, as it is refined by Virgil in the Georgics; and the familiar, epistolary way of Horace." [62]

But in a broader sense—going beyond the propriety of using ancient poets as models for separate parts of the poem—Akenside considers the subject and special intention of the work as a whole to require qualities of style perhaps not necessary for ordinary didactic poems. The pleasures of imagination, he says, "tending almost constantly to admiration and enthusiasm, seemed rather to demand a more open, pathetic, and figured style." [63] And, in general, the social value of such a poem as this is grounded on the poet's special ability to portray God's true reality, and to expose unreality in human affairs, an ability not purely "rational" or "calculative" but also involving spontaneous, "given" qualities and powers.

---

59 II. 175–771.

60 Design, pp. 84–85.

61 III. 78–240.

62 Design, p. 85.

63 *Ibid.* He apparently has Pope's *Essay on Criticism* and *Essay on Man* in mind as poems in which a less "figured," less "pathetic," and less "open" style was called for. It is likely Akenside was indebted both to Thomson's *The Seasons* and to Henry Brooke's *Universal Beauty* (1735) for images and terminology, though not so much for characteristics of versification.

Akenside begins his poem by calling upon the "gentle powers / Of musical delight" [64] to attend him and to bring all the
proper "associates":

> Thou, smiling queen of every tuneful breast,
> Indulgent Fancy! from the fruitful banks
> Of Avon, whence thy rosy fingers cull
> Fresh flowers and dews to sprinkle on the turf
> Where Shakespeare lies, be present: and with thee
> Let Fiction come, upon her vagrant wings
> Wafting ten thousand colours through the air,
> Which, by the glances of her magic eye,
> She blends and shifts at will, thro' countless forms,
> Her wild creation. Goddess of the lyre,
> Which rules the accents of the moving sphere,
> Wilt thou, eternal Harmony! descend
> And join this festive train? for with thee comes
> The guide, the guardian of their lovely sports,
> Majestic Truth; and where Truth deigns to come,
> Her sister Liberty will not be far.
> Be present all ye Genii, who conduct
> The wandering footsteps of the youthful bard,
> New to your springs and shades: who touch his ear
> With finer sounds: who heighten to his eye
> The bloom of Nature, and before him turn
> The gayest, happiest attitude of things.[65]

To invoke such "deities," of course, is to follow an established
poetic convention, which may or may not have any real theoretical significance. And Akenside confesses that it is difficult,
even with such aid, to "paint the finest features of the mind, /
And to most subtile and mysterious things / Give colour,
strength, and motion." [66] He obviously is not presenting here
a doctrine of spontaneous poetic production by divine or nat-

---

[64] I. 6–7.
[65] I. 9–30.
[66] I. 46–48.

ural "possession"; his poet, unlike the Homer of Plato's *Ion*, will need "rational" knowledge of what he is trying to do and of how it must be accomplished, and there is no suggestion that he is incapable of such knowledge.

Nevertheless, within the main body of the poem affirmations of divine inspiration, in one sense or another, are frequent. The characteristic metaphors are highly suggestive. One of Akenside's favorite images is that of breath and breathing, especially as combined with images of fire, flame, or "kindling"; and in this combination it usually implies enlivening and special empowering: [67]

> Oft have the laws of each poetic strain
> The critic-verse employed; yet still unsung
> Lay this prime subject, though importing most
> A poet's name: for fruitless is the attempt,
> By dull obedience and by creeping toil
> Obscure to conquer the severe ascent
> Of high Parnassus. Nature's kindling breath
> Must fire the chosen genius; Nature's hand
> Must string his nerves, and imp his eagle wings
> Impatient of the painful steep, to soar
> High as the summit; there to breathe at large
> Æthereal air: with bards and sages old,
> Immortal sons of praise.[68]

In a later passage he invokes an ancient spirit of wisdom to help him rise to the occasion of the poem:

> Genius of ancient Greece! whose faithful steps
> Well pleas'd I follow through the sacred paths
> Of Nature and of Science; nurse divine
> Of all heroic deeds and fair desires!
> O! let the breath of thy extended praise

---

[67] The "breathing" image also frequently carries the ideas of "speech" and of mental "expression." See, e.g., II. 315–22; III. 400–412.

[68] I. 31–43.

Inspire my kindling bosom to the height
Of this untempted theme.[69]

In a more general, metaphysical context Akenside argues
that the Almighty One imparts the "breath of life" to all living things, and, though some creatures are "temper'd with a
purer flame," [70] all human souls are formed so that "In mortal
bosoms" *burns* an "unquenched hope, / That breathes from
day to day sublimer things." [71] But the fire-breathing image
now changes to one of *gazing* at a fire: who "but rather turns
/ To heaven's broad fire his unconstrained view, / Than to
the glimmering of a waxen flame?" [72] And then, by means of
an easy transition from "broad fire" to "sun," the "form divine" of Beauty herself is said to inspire, by a powerful, life-
giving ray, the poet's verse written in her own praise, and the
central image is now one of "beaming":

> But lo! disclos'd in all her smiling pomp,
> Where Beauty onward moving claims the verse
> Her charms inspire: the freely-flowing verse
> In thy immortal praise, O form divine,
> Smooths her mellifluent stream. Thee, Beauty, thee
> The regal dome, and thy enlivening ray
> The mossy roofs adore: thou, better sun!
> For ever beamest on the enchanted heart
> Love, and harmonious wonder, and delight
> Poetic.[73]

---

[69] I. 567–80. See also, e.g., II. 318–19. In calling upon this "spirit" the poet
is endeavoring to bring to his work not merely the superior artistry of
ancient Greek writers—in the tradition in which Pope, for example, ad-
vocated following both nature and ancient masters—but the wisdom of
their philosophies and the real beauty and virtue of their lives and
society. See I. 595–604.

[70] I. 73–74.

[71] I. 166–68.

[72] I. 174–76.

[73] I. 271–80.

In the "allegory" in Book II, finally, Akenside has the "Genius of human kind," who visited the character Harmodius, state that the Sire Omnipotent has assigned to a sublime and regal "goddess" of true moral beauty the task of inspiring human beings to all their nobler and worthier activities:

> Oft from the radiant honours of his throne,
> He sent whom most he lov'd, the sovereign fair,
> The effluence of his glory, whom he plac'd
> Before his eyes for ever to behold;
> The goddess from whose inspiration flows
> The toil of patriots, the delight of friends;
> Without whose work divine, in heaven or earth,
> Nought lovely, nought propitious comes to pass,
> Nor hope, nor praise, nor honour. Her the Sire
> Gave it in charge to rear the blooming mind,
> The folded powers to open, to direct
> The growth luxuriant of his [the mind's] young desires,
> And from the laws of this majestic world
> To teach him what was good.[74]

It is clear that in Akenside's conception the poet, as a child of Fancy, is eminently in communion with this divine, expressive spirit who raises in him that profound superior pleasure, that love and admiration of God's universe with which he may infuse his poems. The true poet's artistry is, indeed, an enthusiastic and joyous experience, for by its very nature it brings him into a special harmony with the highest manifestations of God's true reality. It is in this sense, if in no other, that the divine form of Beauty—which, at the higher level of being, coalesces with Truth and Virtue—may be said to inspire him, to "beam" on his "enchanted heart" the noble passions of love, wonder, and poetic delight; his fancy is moved by the real expressive, spiritual forms themselves—and these are the true subjects of his poems.

---

[74] II. 377–90.

DIVINE CREATION AND THE MIMIC ART

The ultimate importance, however, of the concepts of "expression" (whether original or from association) and "inspiration" (whether in breathing, firing, or beaming imagery) lies in the fact that they are primary elements in Akenside's description of the creation of the universe. He gives three distinct accounts of divine creation, one in each of the poem's three books. The first is a direct statement of the origin of those objects and powers of imagination which the poem discusses; [75] the second is expressed by the "Genius of human kind" who visits Harmodius in the allegory on the pleasures of the passions; [76] and the third is a brief illustration in the discussion of human mimic art.[77] The three descriptions are not, however, in fundamental conflict.

In the first, God is the "Almighty One" who, prior (in human time) to sun, moon, earth, and human wisdom,

> deep-retir'd
> In his unfathom'd essence, view'd the forms,
> The forms eternal, of created things;
> The radiant sun, the moon's nocturnal lamp,
> The mountains, woods and streams, the rolling globe,
> And Wisdom's mien celestial. From the first
> Of days, on them his love divine he fix'd,
> His admiration: till in time complete,
> What he admir'd and lov'd, his vital smile
> Unfolded into being. Hence the breath
> Of life informing each organic frame,
> Hence the green earth, and wild resounding waves;
> Hence light and shade alternate; warmth and cold;
> And clear autumnal skies and vernal show'rs,
> And all the fair variety of things.[78]

---

[75] I. 56–78.
[76] II. 304–63.
[77] III. 399–403.
[78] I. 64–78.

In the second, much fuller, account, where the "Genius of human kind" is explaining the grounds of the larger justice and beauty of "Providence," God is called the "Sovereign Spirit of the world" who,

> self-collected from eternal time,
> Within his own deep essence . . . beheld
> The bounds of true felicity complete;
> Yet by immense benignity inclin'd
> To spread around him that primeval joy
> Which fill'd himself, he rais'd his plastic arm,
> And sounded through the hollow depths of space
> The strong, creative mandate. Straight arose
> These heavenly orbs, the glad abodes of life,
> Effusive kindled by his breath divine
> Through endless forms of being.[79]

The lines immediately following these further add to, but do not radically conflict with, the view of creation expressed in Book I. Thus, not only was the universe created, but each of its parts

> inhal'd
> From him its portion of the vital flame,
> In measure such, that, from the wide complex
> Of coexistent orders, one might rise,
> One order, all-involving and entire.[80]

It is, moreover, an order corresponding to the best and most beautiful of the many eternal conceptions in God's mind and one in which all the roles and powers of its parts are predetermined and prearranged for the good of the whole:

> He too beholding in the sacred light
> Of his essential reason, all the shapes
> Of swift contingence, all successive ties

---

[79] II. 308–18.
[80] II. 318–22.

Of action propagated through the sum
Of possible existence, he at once,
Down the long series of eventful time,
So fix'd the dates of being, so dispos'd
To every living soul of ev'ry kind
The field of motion and the hour of rest,
That all conspir'd to his supreme design,
To universal good: with full accord
Answering the mighty model he had chose,
The best and fairest of unnumber'd worlds
That lay from everlasting in the store
Of his divine conceptions.[81]

To the first description, then, Akenside's "Genius of human kind" has made some additions: the "creative mandate" was sounded in "the hollow depths of space"; God creates with a "plastic arm"; the one order is established through the common "inhalation" by each of the lower orders of its proper portion of God's "vital flame"; and God is restricted only by his own essential benignant determination to choose the best of his many possible "conceptions." Further, the creative act is something which not only was accomplished—there was a time when the universe was only a possible conception—but also, since the creative mandate sounded, has been continuing:

Nor content,
By one exertion of creative power
His goodness to reveal: through every age,

---

81 II. 323–37. See Note to II, 335; p. 146: "The opinion is so old, that Timaeus Locrus calls the Supreme Being δημιουργὸς τοῦ βελτίονος, the artificer of that which is best; and represents him as resolving in the beginning to produce the most excellent work, and as copying the world most exactly from his own intelligible and essential idea; 'so that it yet remains, as it was at first, perfect in beauty, and will never stand in need of any correction or improvement.' There can be no room for a caution here, to understand the expressions, not of any particular circumstances of human life separately considered, but of the sum or universal system of life and being. See also the vision at the end of the Théodicée of Leibnitz."

Through every moment up the track of time
His parent hand with ever new increase
Of happiness and virtue has adorn'd
The vast harmonious frame: his parent hand,
From the mute shell-fish gasping on the shore,
To men, to angels, to celestial minds
For ever leads the generations on
To higher scenes of being; while supplied
From day to day with his enlivening breath,
Inferior orders in succession rise
To fill the void below.[82]

In the very brief reference to divine creation in Book III, Akenside speaks of a time when

from Chaos old the jarring seeds
Of Nature at the voice divine repair'd
Each to its place, till rosy earth unveil'd
Her fragrant bosom, and the joyful sun
Sprung up the blue serene.[83]

Here he provides the final missing element of the divine creative act: the materials upon which the divine conception was exerted, and out of which the concrete ordered whole was thus constructed. Before the creation of the universe there was a chaos of quasi-Democritean "atoms"[84] swirling in a void, and there was a Supreme Creator who with great benevolence and joy decided to sound the "creative mandate" and then "breathe" his greatest conception into the formless mass. Now there is a concrete universe, an ordered and beautiful whole infused with the divine spirit; and now there is "the energy of life / Kindling the mass with ever active flame."[85] The implication, of course, is that the "Supreme Creator" did not

82 II. 337–50.
83 III. 399–403.
84 I. 515–17.
85 I. 518–19.

himself create the chaos of atoms out of which the universe was wrought. But Akenside actually does not consider this problem. He is concerned only with the creation of that universe in which he lives as an integral part, that specific product of divine mentality and power which can now be observed in all its beauty and grandeur. And although he does not adopt the Platonic principle of the inherent recalcitrance of matter operating in spite of God's benevolent intentions, according to "necessity" (which inevitably renders God's product an imperfect copy of the eternal pattern), the kind of scheme which Akenside provides remains consistent with his general devaluation of mere "material" things and his glorification of the attributes of "mind." He could not look upon matter as essentially divine or upon thought and expression as "material"; the opposition between mind and matter is fundamental, axiomatic. And nothing could be more natural than to identify the divine and superior with mind and the non-divine and inferior with matter. Yet both are essential aspects or conditions of the initial creation of the universe as well as of the continuing creativity which he attributes to the power and wisdom of God.

The significance of all this is that Akenside's description of human "mimic" art turns in large part on the similarity between human acts of artistic production and the divine act of creation. Prior to the child of Fancy's consideration of the material or medium in which his work of mimic art is to become "permanent," Akenside finds him collecting, examining, and combining the various forms of being which he has been given by nature and has acquired through the associative operation of memory. At length,

> Endow'd with all that nature can bestow,
> The child of Fancy oft in silence bends
> O'er these mixt treasures of his pregnant breast
> With conscious pride. From them he oft resolves

> To frame he knows not what excelling things;
> And win he knows not what sublime reward
> Of praise and wonder.[86]

When enough of these forms of being have been collected and stored in his lively mind; when his "plastic powers / Labour for action," and "blind emotions heave / His bosom," and he is "caught" with "loveliest frenzy"; when the multitudes of forms of being, "Like spectres trooping to the wizard's call / Flit swift before him," [87] then begins a hazardous and uncertain process of comparing, blending, dividing, enlarging and extenuating, opposing, ordering, and varying these forms in his mind, from which emerges an ordered conception.

>   With fixed gaze
> He marks the rising phantoms. Now compares
> Their diff'rent forms; now blends them, now divides,
> Enlarges and extenuates by turns;
> Opposes, ranges in fantastic bands,
> And infinitely varies. Hither now,
> Now thither fluctuates his inconstant aim,
> With endless choice perplex'd. At length his plan
> Begins to open. Lucid order dawns;
> And as from Chaos old the jarring seeds
> Of Nature at the voice divine repair'd
> Each to its place . . .
>   by swift degrees
> Thus disentangled, his entire design
> Emerges. Colours mingle, features join,
> And lines converge: the fainter parts retire;
> The fairer eminent in light advance;
> And every image on its neighbour smiles.
> Awhile he stands, and with a father's joy
> Contemplates.[88]

---

86 III. 374–80.
87 III. 380–87.
88 III. 390–410.

He contemplates, that is, the ordered whole *in conception;* and, like the Supreme Creator, he joyously knows that it is this conception which he must, with his "plastic powers," *embody.*

> Then with Promethéan art,
> Into its proper vehicle he breathes
> The fair conception, which embodied thus,
> And permanent, becomes to eyes and ears
> An object ascertain'd.[89]

There are, of course, important differences between the divine and the human creative acts. The most obvious one is that the divine artist breathes his one best conception into the the raw matter of the external universe itself, while the poet works upon the medium of human language. Also, the divine creator began with eternal ideas and an infinite variety of "conceptions" to choose from already in his mind, but the poet begins with potential "seeds" and "powers" which must be "nutured" or developed, and his conception of an ordered whole must *emerge* after a process of fermentation and contemplation. Moreover, the conception with which the poet "informs" his poem, and which gives it such great affective power, is clearly not a product of simple, benevolent choice as it is for the divine creator. The poet is indeed an artist, in the sense that he does not function wholly by divine possession, and Akenside speaks of the vast choice which mimic art has from among all the forms of being presented by the poet's native "sister powers," Fancy and Memory.[90] But he also refers to the "loveliest frenzy"

---

89 III. 410–14.

90 Earlier (I. 9–18) the "sister powers" are Fancy and Fiction, goddesses whom Akenside invokes for aid; "memory" and "fiction" are closely related in Akenside's scheme, since memory is conceived as the basic source from which "imitation" works. The relation between memory and the power of fancy or imagination in general is also very close, since it is upon the material supplied by memory that fancy must work in producing the "secondary" objects and pleasures of imagination.

with which the poet is "caught," and describes the elaborate
process of selecting and ordering the forms of being as "fluc-
tuating" and "inconstant" and "perplex'd" until the plan
itself "begins to open." There is in the poet's art the inevitable human dependence upon something other than one-
self. When he finally makes his creative choice, it is not a
simple, conscious decision to "arrange" given materials into a
certain preconceived order. The order "dawns"; the "light"
of it informs the various parts.

Nevertheless, both God and the poet are by their natures
committed to the best of all possible conceptions; both are
essentially makers of organic wholes, each part of which may
be said to be informed by their controlling "expressive" conceptions; both work in materials already given, into which
they "breathe" their conceptions, imparting to those materials
qualities and values which they could not otherwise possess.
As God gives to swirling atoms order and the "breath of life,"
so the poet may give to his tumbling chaos of imagery and his
language order and a special expressive power. And when the
poet is able to inform his materials with his own "divine" conception, then it is that

> The various organs of his mimic skill . . .
> Beyond their proper powers attract the soul
> By that expressive semblance, while in sight
> Of Nature's great original we scan
> The lively child of Art; while line by line,
> And feature after feature we refer
> To that sublime exemplar whence it stole
> Those animating charms. Thus Beauty's palm
> Betwixt them wavering hangs: applauding Love
> Doubts where to choose; and mortal man aspires
> To tempt creative praise.[91]

---

91 III. 415–27.

Then, in other words, the poem has been given the essential qualities of expressive and creative mind by which the higher values of beauty, truth, and virtue have their prime existence in human experience.

The formulation of the poetic act as analogous to divine creativity provides the ultimate rationale for assigning to the poet his special social and philosophic tasks. This is made finally clear by the resemblance which Akenside draws between the proper activity of the poet and the *continuing* "creativity" of the supreme author. He describes the "living" part of the created universe not as a static order but as a continually "aspiring" one. Each form of life possesses a proper portion of God's "vital flame," and it is natural for each to aspire to a higher level:

> As flame ascends,
> As bodies to their proper centre move,
> As the pois'd ocean to the attracting moon
> Obedient swells, and every headlong stream
> Devolves its winding waters to the main;
> So all things which have life aspire to God,
> The sun of being, boundless, unimpair'd,
> Centre of souls! [92]

In order to "prompt" the creatures to their upward aspiration God has sent "the faithful voice / Of Nature"; but they also receive from the "care of Heaven" the special "aid" they need, "proportioned" to their various "stations," so that all "may persevere / To climb the ascent of being, and approach / For ever nearer to the life divine." [93] The poet, in Akenside's conception, may assume something like God's benevolent role and may design his special offspring to perform a similar task in the society of men. He too is creative in the providential, "continuing" sense that he may strive to encourage the proper

---

92 II. 350–57.
93 II. 357–63.

aspiring movement of the minds of men away from the inferior orders of experience to those higher moral and religious objects designed to be loved and admired. God's means of accomplishing this benevolent purpose include the many "charms" of human and external nature. The true poet not only "steals" these "animating charms," in his act of imitating the divine creator,[94] but also gives them a structure and spirit corresponding to their natural, pre-established aspiring order. And, indeed, Akenside's own poem is designed to portray not only the mere external objects of nature, which please the senses of men, but also the eternal spiritual forms and the divine, expressive "connections" of things by which God has ordered the universe.[95]

Although "the man / Whose eye ne'er open'd on the light of heaven, / Might smile with scorn," declaring that Beauty is but a dream, because "the glooms / Of dulness hang too heavy" on his sense "To let her shine upon" him,[96] and although different minds incline to different objects, nevertheless the "well-tun'd heart"—"blest of Heaven"[97]—enjoys profound and various bliss from "the store / Of Nature [which] fair Imagination culls / To charm the enliven'd soul."[98] Nor is it merely "fresh pleasure" that is enjoyed;

> for the attentive mind,
> By this harmonious action on her powers
> Becomes herself harmonious; wont so oft
> In outward things to meditate the charm
> Of sacred order, soon she seeks at home
> To find a kindred order, to exert
> Within herself this elegance of love,

---

94 III. 423–24.
95 III. 455–64. Cf. his final account of the supremacy of the poet, in *The Pleasures of the Imagination*, Book IV (1770), lines 101–30.
96 III. 448–51.
97 III. 437, 568.
98 III. 572–74.

> This fair-inspir'd delight: her temper'd powers
> Refine at length, and ev'ry passion wears
> A chaster, milder, more attractive mien.[99]

And, further, if the mind extends itself beyond the "lesser graces" of nature to "ampler prospects," assuming "the port / Of that Eternal Majesty that weigh'd / The world's foundations," then will its own change be far "mightier" and nobler.[100]

> Would the forms
> Of servile custom cramp her generous powers?
> Would sordid policies, the barbarous growth
> Of ignorance and rapine, bow her down
> To tame pursuits, to indolence and fear?
> Lo! she appeals to Nature, to the winds
> And rolling waves, the sun's unwearied course,
> The elements and seasons: all declare
> For what the Eternal Maker has ordain'd
> The powers of man: we feel within ourselves
> His energy divine: he tells the heart,
> He meant, he made us to behold and love
> What he beholds and loves, the general orb
> Of life and being; to be great like him,
> Beneficent and active. Thus the men
> Whom Nature's works can charm, with God himself
> Hold converse; grow familiar, day by day,
> With his conceptions, act upon his plan;
> And form to his, the relish of their souls.[101]

What nobler role could be given to the human poet than to awaken and "dispose" the minds of men to these "loveliest" features of the world by means of his own God-like, "charming" acts of expressive, creative, mimic artistry!

---

[99] III. 599–608.
[100] III. 609–15.
[101] III. 616–34.

<4>

Hartley and the Providence
of God

On a First Reading of David Hartley's *Observations on Man* (1749) one may be inclined to think that the two volumes were written by different men from entirely different points of view. One is a "scientific" examination of the "frame" of the human body and mind and "their mutual Connexions and Influences"; the other is an almost evangelistic disquisition on the "duty" and "expectations" of mankind.[1] In his preface Hartley confessed that the work was not composed as a single systematic endeavor but as an attempt to "put together" various papers which he had written at different times, adding "such Things as were necessary to make the Whole appear more complete and systematical."[2] All the ambiguities were certainly not removed in this process, but he says enough about the connection between the two parts to make a general formulation of the work's essential unity possible.

The substance of the first part is developed from a few gen-

---

[1] *Observations on Man, his Frame, his Duty, and his Expectations, in Two Parts* (London, 1749), I, iii; II, iii. Unless otherwise indicated, numerals in references to Hartley indicate part (and volume), proposition number (when appropriate), and pages of the 1749 edition, in that order. The proposition number will facilitate location of the passages in other editions.

[2] Preface, I, v–vi. An interesting account of the "history" of many of these papers is provided indirectly in "The Correspondence of Dr. David Hartley and Rev. John Lister," *Transactions of the Halifax Antiquarian Society* (Halifax, England, 1938), pp. 231–78.

eral laws applied to all the phenomena of human life which Hartley can call to mind; that of the second part is developed mainly by the interaction of these laws and their applications with his largely a priori theological doctrines.[3] Any object of discussion may appear in two "realms" and, accordingly, receive two different treatments: (1) its "actual" nature and behavior and (2) its value, regulation, and destiny in God's ultimate order of things. In Hartley's conception, however, the two schemes are not of equal status; yet neither are they completely different and independent investigations. It may be somewhat surprising to realize that Hartley considers religion, the subject of direct discussion in the second part, to be the highest form of inquiry, to which all other "Branches of Knowlege [sic] ought to be considered as mere Preparatories and Preliminaries," and, conversely, by which all other forms of inquiry or activity ought to be directed.[4] Natural science and philosophy especially are not to be pursued merely for the satisfaction of curiosity.[5] But this in no way means denuding or hampering the intellectual efforts of men: "Those Parts of the Arts and Sciences which bring Glory to God, and Advantage to Mankind, which inspire Devotion, and instruct us how to be useful to others, abound with more and greater Beauties, than such as are profane, mischievous, unprofitable, or minute"; and "the Study of the Scriptures, of Natural History, and Natural Philosophy, of the Frame of the human Mind &c. when undertaken and pursued with benevolent and pious Intentions, lead to more elegant Problems, and surprising Discoveries, than any Study intended for mere private Amusement." [6]

This special task of devoting "science" to the glory of God and to the welfare of others requires the ability to demonstrate resemblance, agreement, and harmony—the "peculiar Charac-

3 See, e.g., Preface, I, vi–viii; Concl. to Part I, pp. 500–512.

4 I. 88, pp. 366–67.

5 I. 87, p. 342.

6 II. 56, p. 245.

teristics of Truth"[7]—between the findings of such "scientific" inquiries and the higher purposes and authority of scriptural and natural religion.[8] Indeed, according to Hartley, philosophical inquiry of any sort, whether secular or religious, must be conducted in terms of a scale of perfect and imperfect "agreement," and the process of association itself is essentially one of building by "mutual connexions" among sensations and ideas of things. Moreover, "analogy" and "association" are sometimes interchangeable expressions.[9] Hartley distinguishes among three ascending orders of "agreement" of ideas: "analogy," partial "induction," and perfect "coalescence." The first two correspond roughly to what on some occasions he calls "imperfect" analogy between our ideas of things in nature. The third (also called "the highest Kind of Induction") is the sort of intuitive "coincidence" of ideas which occurs only in mathematics. Agreement of ideas in general, however, is the principal criterion of truth—or ground for "assent." [10] All agreement, perfect and imperfect, is an instrument of science, for progress in knowledge is obtained by application of prior truths to new instances,[11] and it is often

---

[7] II. 13, p. 52.

[8] See Preface, I, vii–viii; Introd. to Part II, pp. 3–4; I. 88, pp. 366–67.

[9] In his attempt, for example, to prove the historical truth of the miracles recorded in the Christian scriptures (as part of his elaborate proof of the "Truth of the Christian Religion"), he moves to put the whole matter in a "more natural, as well as a more philosophical Light," in terms of his basic analysis of the human mind, in which the proper grounds of truth (or human "assent") are set forth: "Assocation, *i.e.* Analogy, perfect and imperfect, is the only Foundation upon which we in fact do, or can, or ought to assent; and consequently a Dissonance from Analogy, or Repugnancy thereto, is a necessary Foundation for Dissent. . . . Now the Progress of the human Mind, as may be seen by all the Inquiries into it, and particularly by the History of Association, is a Thing of a determinate Nature; a Man's Thoughts, Words, and Actions, are all generated by something previous; there is an established Course for these things, an Analogy, of which every Man is a Judge from what he feels in himself, and sees in others" (II. 28, p. 146).

[10] I. 87, pp. 341–45.

[11] Part I, p. 6.

necessary to exert these prior truths upon new phenomena on the basis of only partial or imperfect likeness of ideas instead of perfect "coalescence." Hartley asserts that the "analogous Natures of all the Things about us, are a great Assistance in decyphering their Properties, Powers, Laws, &c. inasmuch as what is minute or obscure in one may be explained and illustrated by the analogous Particular in another, where it is large and clear. And thus all Things become Comments on each other in an endless Reciprocation." [12] Thus when "there are various Arguments for the same Thing taken from Induction or Analogy, they may all be considered as supporting one another in the same manner as independent Evidences"; [13] "the great Business in all Branches of Knowlege is thus to reduce, unite, and simplify our Evidences; so as that the one resulting Proof, by being of a higher Order, shall be more than equal in Force to all the concurrent ones of the inferior Orders." [14]

It is by means of this broadly analogical process that he attempts to perform his thoroughgoing reduction of human behavior to the principle of association; and he is able to argue further not only that revealed and natural religion mutually support one another, but also that the truth of the scriptures (about which, of course, there is no real doubt) can be "proved" almost entirely from their agreement with the human mind, with true principles of style and manner for such writing, with history, natural and civil, with themselves, and with "natural" moral excellence.[15] But the larger consequence

---

12 I. 87, p. 343.

13 *Ibid.* Cf. I. 82, pp. 293–97, where "analogy" is defined and discussed separately.

14 I. 87, pp. 344–45. Cf. p. 351: "It appears also not impossible that future Generations should put all Kinds of Evidences and Inquiries into mathematical Forms; and, as it were, reduce Aristotle's ten Categories, and Bishop *Wilkin's* forty *Summa Genera,* to the Head of Quantity alone, so as to make Mathematics and Logic, Natural History, and Civil History, Natural Philosophy, and Philosophy of all other Kinds, coincide *omni ex parte.*"

15 See II. 22, 24, 25, 28, 34, pp. 97–98, 104–22, 122–26, 146, 167–72.

of this principle of agreement, coupled with the principle of the primacy of religion, is that unlike an "associationist" and "experimental" philosopher such as Hume, Hartley demands the ability to see not only the peculiar characteristics and laws of various things in nature, but also, and more importantly, the grounds and character of their common participation in God's universal order and plan.

Hence there is no inevitable contradiction between at least the basic schemes of the two parts of Hartley's work; in fact, once the dialectical interaction is effected, there is no simple line of demarcation between them. The characteristics of a thing that may be singled out for attention in the "actual" or "behavioral" treatment of Part One naturally reflect the more general "desiderative" or "ideal" treatment presented in Part Two; at the same time the latter treatment both reflects and presupposes the results of the former.[16] The "mutual connexions" between religion and other human affairs, however, are to be decided finally in relation to the better and ultimate religious criteria. The peculiarities of the various arts and sciences, though in one sense real, must be either assimilated to or transcended in terms of the objectives and laws of religion, natural and revealed. Thus in describing his own work, Hartley not only asserts that contemplation of the "frame" of man will contribute directly to the study of true religion, but also declares openly his religious motives: "Now, the Contemplation of our own Frame and Constitution appears to me to have a peculiar Tendency to lessen . . . [some] Difficulties attending Natural and Revealed Religion, and to improve their Evidences, as well as to concur with them in their Determination of Man's Duty and Expectations. With this View, I drew up the foregoing Observations on the Frame and Connexion of the Body and Mind." [17]

The character of Hartley's own pious and benevolent study

---

[16] See, e.g., II. 12, p. 48; II. 71, p. 313.
[17] Introd. to Part II, p. 3.

of the "frame" and "connexion" of the human body and mind may perhaps best be explained by reference to the familiar doctrine of fallen man, the main substance of which he assumes as unquestionable and as prior in being (if not in knowledge) to all mental and bodily processes.[18] This basic description of man is *presupposed* in the psychologistic analysis in Part One, and that analysis, with its quasi-materialism, sensationism, and overtly mechanical principle of association, is thus of an essentially inferior and dependent creature, one that has fallen out of a higher, innocent, spiritual paradise and is now in a treacherous, though not completely hopeless, state of trial and transition. Hartley clearly is not attempting (in the manner of Hume) to introduce into the realm of morality an experimental method to establish the nature of human good and evil or beauty and deformity on the basis of actual human approbation and blame. He is attempting rather (somewhat in the manner of the Reverend John Gay) [19] to

---

18 It would be difficult to overestimate the significance of this doctrine in Hartley's system. Even the quarrelings of men over questions of religion and morality themselves can be referred to the general inferior condition into which mankind plunged at the Fall: "We ought to lay it down as certain, that this Perplexity and Uneasiness commenced with the Fall, with the Eating of the Fruit of the Tree of the Knowlege of Good and Evil; and that it can never be intirely removed till our Readmission to Paradise, and to the Tree whose Leaves are for *the Healing of the Nations*. We must expect therefore, that, though humble and pious Inquiries will always be attended with some Success and Illumination, still much Darkness and Ignorance will remain" (II. 61, p. 257). For Hartley's view of the consequences, both good and evil, of the confusion of tongues at Babel, see I. 83, pp. 297–315; I. 86, pp. 333–34; I. 2, p. 9.

19 "Dissertation Concerning the Fundamental Principle of Virtue or Morality" (prefixed to Edmund Law's translation [1731] of William King's *De origine mali* [1702–1704]). Hartley announced that Gay's assertion of the "Possibility of deducing all our intellectual Pleasures and Pains from Association" was the initial impetus for his own work (Preface, I, v). Gay's treatise is available in L. A. Selby-Bigge, ed., *British Moralists* (Oxford, 1897), II, 267–85. It seems likely that Hartley was also strongly influenced by Ralph Cudworth, Samuel Clarke, and Joseph Butler; adequate exploration of this question has never been attempted, perhaps largely because

understand this fallen creature whose mind operates mechanically by association of simple sensations, and perhaps by material particles vibrating in its medullary substance, in order to ascertain better how its natural *behavior* can be regulated according to the rules of *conduct* revealed by God.

In this program, Hartley seems unwilling to decide upon the exact nature of human ideas and the soul or to choose among a number of available explanations of the relationship between the natural motions of the brain and the sensations arising in the soul.

> ... for it is all one to the Purpose of the foregoing Theory, whether the Motions in the medullary Substance be the physical Cause of the Sensations, according to the System of the Schools; or the occasional Cause, according to *Malbranche;* or only an Adjunct, according to *Leibnitz.* However, this is not supposing Matter to be endued with Sensation, or any way explaining what the Soul is; but only taking its Existence, and Connexion with the bodily Organs in the most simple Case, for granted, in order to make farther Inquiries.
> ... I would not therefore be any-way interpreted so as to oppose the Immateriality of the Soul.

At the same time, he points out candidly, the various arguments that have been offered for the "immateriality" of the human soul are not completely convincing.[20]

Nevertheless, he does not doubt that the human soul can acquire something "spiritual," and he is not hesitant about the superiority of the spiritual over the material; "the future Happiness of the Good" (their temporary paradisiacal existence after death) will probably be "of a spiritual Nature";[21]

---

of the widespread tendency to classify Hartley with the "experimental" associationists (in Hume's sense) and materialists. The Reverend John Gay was, in any case, far from being an "experimental" associationist in moral theory.

20 Concl. to Part I, pp. 511–12.

21 II. 89, p. 397.

the final kingdom of Christ will be a spiritual one; [22] and God, the supreme cause of all things, is a spiritual being.[23] Moreover, one of our crucial practical problems is to avoid the "carnal" pleasures, to rise from the "carnal" and sensual toward the spiritual joys. Only those carnal pleasures which seem to have been designed for the propagation of the race and for the maintenance of others (in marriage) are permitted (they are not required)—though even these natural pleasures remain, ironically, "Marks of our fallen State." [24] Fortunately, however, God has so ordered the ruins of Paradise that the law of association itself tends naturally to aid us in our task of avoiding the carnal: "Some Degree of Spirituality is the necessary Consequence of passing through Life. The sensible Pleasures and Pains must be transferred by Association more and more every Day, upon Things that afford neither sensible Pleasure nor sensible Pain in themselves, and so beget the

---

22 II. 53, p. 234. This is one of the topics on which Hartley debated with his friend the Reverend John Lister in the years preceding the publication of *Observations on Man*. Lister resisted Hartley's doctrine of the ultimate inevitability of virtue and happiness for *all* mankind at some distant future time (the final kingdom); the question of whether a man's "temporary" existence after death could be wholly spiritual was also raised. See *Transactions of the Halifax Antiquarian Society*, 1938, pp. 234–38, 245–51.

23 II. 6, pp. 31–34.

24 II. 53, p. 234. See General Corollaries to Sections 2–8, ch. iii, part I, pp. 341–46; II. 76, pp. 347–58; and II. 86–95, pp. 382–437. Christians, of course, naturally tend to approach a higher degree of spirituality than earlier man ("the Patriarchs and Jews"); for, since Christians "live in the more adult Ages of Mankind," they have "stricter Precepts, and are obliged to higher Degrees of Spirituality, as . . . [they] approach nearer to the spiritual Kingdom of Christ" (II. 53, p. 234). But more generally the "rule of life" for all mankind, Christian and heathen alike, demands that all human pleasures and pains—from mere sensation up to the initial responses of the moral sense—ultimately be regulated by the proper precepts and examples of benevolence and piety. And Hartley is convinced, on scriptural grounds, that before that final day when all men are made happy again in God, the future punishment of the wicked and the future happiness of the good will be infinite, "in that real practical Sense to which alone our Conceptions extend" (Preface, I, viii).

intellectual Pleasures and Pains." Since our transitional life
has been arranged so that our sensible pleasures somewhat out-
number our sensible pains, "Association . . . has a Tendency
to reduce the State of those who have eaten of the Tree of the
Knowlege of Good and Evil, back again to a paradisiacal
one." [25]

It is, of course, only a tendency. But the fallen human world
as Hartley perceives it is not a system of manifest cruelty or
vengeance; it "is a System of Benevolence, and consequently
its Author the Object of unbounded Love and Adoration." [26]
Although human life is not an ultimate form of existence, and
is naturally fraught with confusion, error, sin, and folly,
Hartley can still take an essentially optimistic attitude in his
benevolent and pious attempt to set forth the frame, duty,
and expectations of man.

> Whatever be our Doubts, Fears, or Anxieties, whether
> selfish or social, whether for Time or Eternity, our only
> Hope and Refuge must be in the infinite Power, Knowlege,
> and Goodness of God. And if these be really our Hope and
> Refuge, if we have a true practical Sense and Conviction of
> God's infinite Ability and Readiness to protect and bless us,
> an intire, peaceful, happy Resignation will be the Result,
> notwithstanding the Clouds and Perplexities wherewith we
> may sometimes be encompassed. He who has brought us into
> this State, will conduct us through it: He knows all our
> Wants and Distresses: His infinite Nature will bear down all
> Opposition from our Impotence, Ignorance, Vice, or Misery:
> He is our Creator, Judge, and King, our Friend, and Father,
> and God.
>
> And though the transcendent Greatness and Gloriousness
> of this Prospect may, at first View, make our Faith stagger,
> and incline us to disbelieve through Joy; yet, upon farther
> Consideration, it seems rather to confirm and establish itself

25 I. 14, pp. 82–83.
26 II. 56, p. 245.

on that Account; for the more it exceeds our Gratitude and Comprehension, the more does it coincide with the Idea of that absolutely perfect Being, whom the several Orders of imperfect Beings perpetually suggest to us, as our only Restingplace, the Cause of Causes, and the supreme Reality.[27]

In Hartley's scheme, of course, the familiar dialectical oppositions—appearance and reality, matter (or sensation) and spirit, opinion and knowledge, becoming and being—are all resolved more negatively than positively; that is, the possibility is not provided that man, by his own efficiency, may rise completely, in this or any other life, from the lower to the higher level. Man was separated from the higher order of things at the Fall, and will be reunited with it by God in His own good time.[28] This helps to explain, for example, why hu-

---

[27] Introd. to Part II, pp. 1–2.

[28] Basil Willey (*Eighteenth Century Background* [London, 1940], pp. 142–44) considerably distorts Hartley's theology in his attempt to present his system as an instance of the so-called eighteenth-century doctrine of benevolent Nature working by an automatic mechanism toward the perfection of man. Hartley holds no such position: "It would be a sufficient Answer to the πόθεν τὸ κακὸν, to all our Difficulties and Anxieties from the Folly, Vice, and Misery, which we experience in ourselves, and see in others, to say, that they will all end in unbounded Knowlege, Virtue, and Happiness; and that the Progress of every Individual in his Passage through an eternal Life is from imperfect to perfect, particular to general, less to greater, finite to infinite, and from the Creature to the Creator.

"But, alas! this is chiefly Speculation, and must be to the Bulk of Mankind. Whilst we continue entangled in the Fetters of Sin, we cannot enjoy the glorious Liberty and Privileges of the Children of God. We cannot exalt ourselves to Heaven, and make a right Estimate of Things, from the true Point of View, till we get clear of the Attraction, and magic Influences, of the Earth. . . . When we view the Sin and Wickedness, with which the World everywhere abounds, our Hearts cannot but melt with Compassion for others, for the Tortures that are prepared for them, after the Expiration of this Life, in order to fit them for pure and spiritual Happiness, to burn out the Stains of Sensuality and Self-love, and exalt them to the unbounded Love of God, and his Works. When we consider farther, that God has Mercy on whom he will, and hardens whom he will, and that we, with all our Pleasures and Pains, are absolute Nothings in comparison of him, we must . . . fall down at his Feet dead with Astonishment. And yet we need

man "truth" is more clearly a matter of "agreement" and "harmony" of ideas than of correspondence to absolute reality. And yet, although the divine scriptures are not presented explicitly as a "substitute" for the "book of the world" which originally functioned to lead man directly from a knowledge of created things to God but which was "destroyed" after the Fall,[29] actual sensible nature is said to reflect the tenets and beings of true religion, and it is partly by the revealed light of the scriptures that the phenomena of nature (including the frame and constitution of man) can be properly perceived as reflections of God, his greatness, and his plan; the "Scriptures are the only Book which can give us any just Idea of antient Times, of the Original of Mankind, their Dispersion, &c. or of what will befal them in future Generations."[30] Because we have been given both the world of nature and the scriptures, a better-worse dialectic is possible in this fallen state in terms of the closeness of our approximation to the higher reality　to ultimate knowledge, spirituality, and existence. For the attributes of the higher reality may be reflected to some extent in human piety and love and their moral and intellectual fruits. We may approximate the "unbounded Knowlege, Virtue, and Happiness" that await us in the final kingdom if, God willing, we prepare ourselves for it with an appropriate pious resignation to our present state. Thus it is that the law of association, by which our ideas, habits, and actions are developed, is made to serve the higher law, the will and glory of God.

When Men have entered sufficiently into the Ways of Piety, God appears more and more to them in the whole Course

---

not fear; from the Instant that we thus humble ourselves, he will lay his Hand upon us, and exalt us; he has the Keys of Death and Hell, in every possible Sense of those Words" (Concl. to Part II, pp. 438–40).

[29] Cf., e.g., Bonaventura, *Itinerarium Mentis ad Deum* i. 6–15 (tr. G. Boas: *The Mind's Road to God* [New York, 1953], pp. 9–13). See McKeon, *Thought, Action, and Passion*, pp. 125, 244–46.

[30] I. 88, p. 366.

and Tenor of their Lives; and by uniting himself with all
their Sensations, and intellectual Perceptions, overpowers all
the Pains; augments, and attracts to himself, all the Pleasures. Everything sweet, beautiful, or glorious, brings in the
Idea of God, mixes with it, and vanishes into it. For all is
God's; he is the only Cause and Reality; and the Existence
of everything else is only the Effect, Pledge, and Proof, of his
Existence and Glory.[31]

ASSOCIATION, INVENTION, AND THE PRECEPTS OF RELIGION

Hartley's first discussion of poetry occurs in Part One in his
detailed consideration of the pleasures and pains of imagination. This class of "intellectual" pleasures and pains, which
are the next remove above the pleasures and pains of sensation,[32] arise in general from "natural or artificial Beauty or
Deformity." [33] They may be analyzed under seven specific
heads: the pleasures arising from (1) natural beauty; (2)
"works of art" (that is, the practical or useful arts of architecture, furniture, and machinery); (3) the "liberal arts" of music,
painting, and poetry; (4) the sciences; (5) the beauty of the
person; (6) wit and humor; and (7) the pains arising from
gross absurdity, inconsistency, or deformity. These are basic
distinctions, but Hartley's procedure is to account for one
pleasure or pain in terms of any or all of the other "intellectual" ones (ambition, self-interest, sympathy, "theopathy,"
and the moral sense) as well as in terms of other pleasures or
pains of imagination—using them all as possible "sources" of
ideas and affections. He recognizes that this might seem to result in elaborate circularity, and, accordingly, he grounds all
the sources of human ideas, when thus treated in terms of the
natural behavior of man, on the singularly stable basis of sensation.

---

[31] II. 71, p. 313.
[32] II. 55, p. 244.
[33] Introd. to Part I, pp. 2–3.

Now it will be a sufficient Proof, that all the intellectual Pleasures and Pains are deducible ultimately from the sensible ones, if we can shew of each intellectual Pleasure and Pain in particular, that it takes its Rise from other Pleasures and Pains, either sensible or intellectual. For thus none of the intellectual Pleasures and Pains can be original. But the sensible Pleasures and Pains are evidently Originals. They are therefore the only ones, *i.e.* they are the common Source from whence all the intellectual Pleasures and Pains are ultimately derived.[34]

The common faculties and habits of the human mind are for the most part passive receptacles. That is, although they must have certain natural capacities and functions, they are, in each individual man, dependent for their special content and character upon the sensations and associations which they happen to receive.[35] A natural "instinct" already oriented toward specific qualities, ideas, or actions is in Hartley's view the prevailing characteristic of brutes, not of men.[36] Hence, for example, the properly developed moral sense, which is the highest and most inclusive class of intellectual pleasures and pains, is more clearly a product of an accumulation of proper associations than an instinctive predisposition toward a special conception of virtue.[37] It is not surprising, therefore, that Hartley refers the pleasures of the liberal arts not to "inner senses" but to the pleasurable ideas such objects can call forth because of their associations in our minds with things outside the liberal arts as such as well as outside the whole realm of imagination.

The "Beauties and Excellencies of good Poetry" (its natural tendency to produce delight in human beings) may be deduced to begin with from three immediate, "intrinsic" sources:

---

34 I. pp. 416–17. See also I. 11, p. 72; Concl. to Part I, p. 503. Cf. *Transactions of the Halifax Antiquarian Society*, 1938, p. 236.

35 See Introd. to Part I, p. 2–3; I, pp. 416–17.

36 See I. 93, pp. 404–15.

37 I. 99, pp. 497–99.

(1) the harmony, variety, and regularity of meter and rhyme, (2) the "Fitness and Strength" of the language, (3) the "Subject-matter of the poem, and the Invention and Judgment exerted by the Poet, in regard to his Subject." The "beauties" of each "are much transferred upon the other Two by Association." [38] But the pleasures from all three elements are controlled by our associations with "other" things. Thus, for example, the explanation of the effect of "figurative words" turns upon a principle of apparent impropriety, in terms of our prior associations:

> Now figurative Words seem to strike and please us chiefly from that Impropriety which appears at first Sight, upon their Application to the Things denoted by them, and from the consequent Heightening of the Propriety, as soon as it is duly perceived. For when figurative Words have recurred so often as to excite the secondary Idea instantaneously, and without any previous Harshness to the Imagination, they lose their peculiar Beauty and Force; and, in order to recover this, and make ourselves sensible of it, we are obliged to recal the literal Sense, and to place the literal and figurative Senses close together, that so we may first be sensible of the Inconsistency, and then be more affected with the Union and Coalescence.[39]

Beyond this, "figurative Expressions illuminate our Discourses and writings by transferring the Properties, Associations, and Emotions, belonging to one Thing upon another, by augumenting, diminishing, &c." When the figures are

> too distant, or too obscure, when they augment or diminish too much, we are displeased; and the principal Art in the Use of Figures is, to heighten, as far as the Imagination will permit, the greatest Beauty lying upon the Confines of what

---

[38] I. 94, p. 428.

[39] *Ibid.*, p. 429. See also his general account of the nature of figurative language, I. 82, pp. 291–97.

disgusts by being too remote or bombast. And this extreme
Limit for figurative Expressions shews evidently, that the
Pleasure arising from them is nearly allied to Pain; and their
Beauty owing to a certain Kind and Degree of Inconsist-
ency.[40]

However, since the figures used in speaking and writing have
great influence on each other and are "much altered" in their
comparative "energy" by our passions, customs, opinions, constitutions, and educations,

> there can be no fixed Standard for determining what is
> Beauty here, or what is the Degree of it. Every person may
> find, that his Taste in these Things receives considerable
> Changes in his Progress through Life; and may, by careful
> Observation, trace up these Changes to the Associations that
> have caused them. And yet, since Mankind have a general
> Resemblance to each other, both in their internal Make, and
> external Circumstances, there will be some general Agree-
> ments about these Things common to all Mankind. The
> Agreements will also become perpetually greater, as the Per-
> sons under Consideration are supposed to agree more in
> their Genius, Studies, external Circumstances, &c. Hence
> may be seen, in part, the Foundation of the general Agree-
> ments observable in Critics, concerning the Beauties of
> Poetry, as well as that of their particular Disputes and Dif-
> ferences.[41]

The pleasure received "from the Matter of the Poem, and
the Invention and Judgment of the Poet, in this [subject mat-
ter] respect," arises primarily from the "real" things which the
poet describes or represents, not from the imitation as such.

> It is necessary therefore, that the Poet should choose such
> Scenes as are beautiful, terrible, or otherwise strongly affect-

---

[40] I. 94, pp. 429–30.
[41] *Ibid.*, p. 430. On the general resemblances and differences among mankind
see also I. 14, p. 82.

ing, and such Characters as excite Love, Pity, just Indigna-
tion, &c.; or rather, that he should present us with a proper
Mixture of all these. For, as they will all please singly, so a
well-ordered Succession of them will much enhance these
separate Pleasures, by the Contrasts, Analogies, and Coinci-
dences, which this may be made to introduce. In all these
Things the chief Art is to copy Nature so well, and to be so
exact in all the principal Circumstances relating to Actions,
Passions, &c. *i.e.* to real Life, that the Reader may be insensibly betrayed into a half Belief of the Truth and Reality of
the Scene.[42]

In Hartley's conception, however, the poetic process of copying nature is not one simply of describing actual historical
things in their original order; it is more a process of re-com-
bining and of "inventing." Poetry, indeed, "and all fictitious
History, borrow one chief Part of their Influence from their
being Imitations of real History, as this again does from the
strong Affections and Passions excited by the Events of Life,
and from the Contagiousness of our Tempers and Disposi-
tions." [43] But poetry is fiction; it involves the inventive processes of producing such ideas as are themselves naturally affective, but without regard for their original order in memory,
and of giving them a form or structure which in a general way
copies real history. Oratory and history are "real," but poetry
is fictitious in the sense that the poet invents the order of parts
or the specific scenes, characters, and events—or both. Poetry
ordinarily has an affective advantage over real history and
oratory in its use of the artificial beauties of figures and numbers, but oratory (at least for some readers) has an advantage
over poetry in being real rather than fictitious.[44] The com-

---

42 I. 94, pp. 430–31.
43 *Ibid.*, p. 432. Although he does not include them in his initial list of
human "faculties" (Introd. to Part I, p. 3), "contagion" and "imitation"
(in an essentially non-literary sense) are both fundamental principles in
Hartley's scheme; and both seem to be primitive, rather than *acquired*
(by association). See, e.g., I. 21, p. 107; I. 77, pp. 256–63; I. 98, p. 490.
44 I. 94, p. 432.

bined force of the figures and the naturally affective subject matter of poetry is especially great. The poet characteristically uses similes, fables, parables, and allegories, which "are all Instances of natural Analogies improved and set off by Art"; and "the Properties, Beauties, Perfections, Desires, or Defects and Aversions, which adhere by Association to the Simile, Parable, or Emblem of any Kind, are insensibly, as it were, transferred upon the Thing represented." [45]

The poet's "invention," by which the fictitious affective subject matter is produced, is defined as a power of producing "new Beauties in Works of Imagination" [46]—in works, that is, which are wrought out of those particularly vivid ideas called up "without regard to the Order of former actual Impressions and Perceptions." The faculty of imagination differs from that of memory, by which ideas are called up "in the same Order and Proportion, accurately or nearly, as they were once actually presented"; [47] but "Copiousness and Quickness of the Invention" is something different from a powerful imagination. A full and quick invention entails a combination of powers: (1) "A strong and quick Memory" (so that "the Ideas . . . may depend upon, and be readily suggested by, each other"), (2) "a large Stock" of the kinds of ideas proper to the task of writing "fictitious histories," and (3) the "Habit of forming and pursuing Analogies, the Deviations from these, and the subordinate Analogies visible in many of these first Deviations." The last of these, the power of analogy, is especially important; in fact, it is this, rather than either imagination or memory, which enables the poet to be specifically "inventive" and not merely imitative of prior literary models.

Analogy will lead him by degrees, in works of Fancy, from the Beauties of celebrated Masters to others [i.e., to other beauties] less and less resembling these, till at last he arrives

---

45 I. 82, p. 297.
46 I. 94, p. 434.
47 Introd. to Part I, p. 3.

at such as bear no visible Resemblance. Deviations, and the
subordinate Analogies contained within them, will do this
in much greater Degree; and all Analogies will instruct him
how to model properly such intirely-new Thoughts, as his
Memory and Acquaintance with Things have suggested to
him.[48]

And of course it is also by his power of analogy that the poet
produces his "figures"—his allegories, parables, and "em-
blems." Hartley does not draw any special connection between "imagination" as a "faculty" and the powers necessary
for poetic production; the imagination is involved in a great
variety of human pursuits, of which poetry is only one. Certainly, the imagination is not *the* poetic power. For that matter, "invention" too is not confined to poets, musicians, or
painters, and he does not hesitate to conclude finally that its
basic nature "seems as reconcileable with, and deducible from,
the Power of Association, and the Mechanism of the Mind
here explained, as that of any other." [49]

Up to this point the analysis directly extends only to the
how and the why of the common natural behavior of human
beings. The second part of *Observations on Man* primarily
concerns not how man "behaves," but how, according to the
precepts of true religion, natural and revealed, he must "conduct" himself. The essential "nature" of poetry—the laws
governing its production and effects—having been established,
now its proper evaluation and regulation according to the
will of God can be made clear. The order of evaluation must
be from the observed moral and affective qualities of poetry,
and the necessity of regulating those qualities, to judgments
concerning the production of those pleasures (and pains)
which lead most directly to the betterment of man. In other
words, the psychologistic analysis of the effects and faculties

---

48 I. 94, pp. 434–35.
49 *Ibid.,* p. 435.

of poetry serves as a requisite preliminary to the task of proper evaluation and regulation both of poetry itself and of the tastes and judgments of its readers. Hence Hartley concludes his treatment of the "actual" nature (or "history") of the pleasures of imagination with a preview of the discussion that is to follow:

> We may now observe upon the Whole, that according to the foregoing History of the Pleasures of Imagination, there must be great Differences in the Tastes and Judgments of different Persons; and that no Age, Nation, Class of Men, &c. ought to be made the Test of what is most excellent in artificial Beauty; nor consequently of what is absurd. The only Things that can be set up as natural Criterions here seem to be Uniformity with Variety, Usefulness in general, and the particular Subserviency of this or that artificial Beauty to improve the Mind, so as to make it suit best with our present Circumstances, and future Expectations. How all these Criterions consist with each other, and unite in the single Criterion of Religion, or the Love of God, and of our Neighbour, understood in the comprehensive Sense of these Words, I shall endeavour to shew hereafter.[50]

As applied specifically to poetry, the religious criterion turns out to have reference to two main Platonic problems: the relation of poetry to reality and the role of poetry in the body social. Poetry is an art of "fiction" that makes "unreal" objects out of naturally affective parts; it "imitates" real history in the sense that it orders ideas of human events, characters, and scenes into sequences which do not derive from mere memory, and its objective must be to make readers half believe that they are witnessing actual events as recorded in histories—that is, to copy nature accurately both in the parts and in the kind of sequence they are given. It is probable, however, that all human inventions, including those of the

---

50 *Ibid.*, p. 442.

philosopher, fall short of the true reality of God, whose "infinite Nature seems strongly to argue, that Existence, Power, Knowlege, and Goodness, do really and properly belong to him alone; and that what we call so here on Earth, in our first and literal Senses, are mere Shadows and Figures of the true Realities." [51] Therefore, when Hartley speaks positively of the "reality" of oratory and history and the "unreality" of poetry, he is referring to the "reality" which we commonly apprehend with our inferior faculties, the images or ideas of which are "real" or "unreal" only in a loose common sense. Ideas of the class of the "pleasures and pains of imagination" are complex and derived, and it is possible to distinguish those which derive directly from historical events or actually existing things (real) from those which derive from recollection and reorganization of our simple sensations and of our ideas of historical events and existing things and their various analogies and differences (unreal). The fact nevertheless remains that even the so-called real ideas do not obviously correspond to *ultimate* reality; and the poet is thus seen as producing, as it were, "imitations of imitations." We can be certain a priori of the infinite superiority of the real transcendent world, as known by God, but its attributes are beyond our powers of depiction or description:

> There is not an Atom perhaps in the whole Universe, which does not abound with Millions of Worlds; and conversly [sic], this great System of the Sun, Planets, and fixed Stars, may be no more than a single constituent Particle of some Body of an immense relative Magnitude, &c. In like manner, there is not a Moment of Time so small, but it may include Millions of Ages in the Estimation of some Beings; and, conversly, the largest Cycle which human Art is able to invent, may be no more than the Twinkling of an Eye in that of others, &c. The infinite Divisibility and Extent of Space and

---

[51] II. 11, p. 43.

Time admit of such Infinites upon Infinites, ascending and descending, as make the Imagination giddy, when it attempts to survey them. But, however this be, we may be sure, that the true System of Things is infinitely more transcendent in Greatness and Goodness, than any Description or Conception of ours can make it.[52]

Further, in connection with the "Elegancies and Amusements of Life" (the "artificial Beauties of Houses, Gardens, Dress, &c."), Hartley establishes a remarkably Platonic hierarchy of value: the undepictable beauties of God and Heaven, the beauties of nature, and the beauties of artificial things. It is clear, he observes,

> that the Beauties of Nature are far superior to all artificial ones, *Solomon in all his Glory not being arrayed like a Lily of the Field.* . . . Even the Beauties of *Nature* are much chequered with Irregularities and Deformities, this World being only the Ruins of a Paradisiacal one. We must not therefore expect intire Order and Perfection in it, till we have passed through the Gate of Death, and are arrived at our Second Paradisiacal State, till Heavens and Earth, and all Things in them, be made anew. How much less then can we hope for Perfection in the Works of human Art! [53]

The main significance of this apparently drastic devaluation of human art derives from the principle that man must have as his chief aim in this life the attainment of piety and virtue. Anything not inherently conducive to these qualities may be studied or pursued (secondarily) only if it can be brought under the rule of the precepts of benevolence, piety, and the moral sense.[54] Hartley separates the pleasures of sensation, imagination, ambition, and self-interest as a group in clear dialectical fashion from the higher group of sympathy,

---

[52] II. 56, pp. 247–48.
[53] II. 57, p. 249.
[54] II. 56, p. 245–48.

theopathy, and the moral sense, even though he maintains at the same time that a better and a worse state or form of each of the lower pleasures can be conceived in terms of the influence of the higher precepts.[55] He does not speak of the "precepts" of sensation, imagination, ambition, or self-interest, only of those of sympathy (benevolence), theopathy (piety), and the moral sense. The pleasures of the lower group cannot have "precepts" allotted especially to them, according to their peculiar ways of operating among human beings; for they are inherently inferior kinds of phenomena (whose "natural" laws therefore provide no inherent proper guide or criterion for them). Furthermore, evaluation of things in general is the special province of the laws of religion, not of the peculiar arts or pleasures of men.[56] Hartley contends, in fact, that uncontrolled study or pursuit, for example, of the liberal arts actually breeds vices of various sorts. "It is evident, that most Kinds of Music, Painting, and Poetry, have close Connexions with Vice, particularly with the Vices of Intemperance and Lewdness; that they represent them in gay, pleasing Colours, or, at least, take off from the Abhorrence due to them." They introduce "a Frame of Mind, quite opposite to that of Devotion, and earnest Concern for our own and others future Welfare." Moreover, a person "cannot acquire any great Skill in these Arts, either as a Critic, or a Master of them, without a great Consumption of Time: They are very apt to excite Vanity, Self-conceit, and mutual Flatteries, in their Votaries; and, in many Cases, the Expense of Fortunes is too considerable to be reconciled to the Charity and Beneficence due to the Indigent." [57] Wit and humor (the essential ingredients of poetry when it takes a light and comic turn), even when free

---

[55] See also his conceptions of the "higher" pleasures of honor (which falls under the natural head of "ambition") and "refined" and "rational" self-interest: II. 63, 65, pp. 262–64, 271–80; I. 96, pp. 458–70.

[56] See, e.g., II. 14, pp. 54–55.

[57] II. 59, pp. 253–54.

from their usual tendency to be mixed with profanity, are especially dangerous; they

> beget a Levity and Dissipation of Mind, that are by no Means consistent with that Seriousness and Watchfulness which are required in Christians, surrounded with Temptations, and yet aiming at Perfection. . . . Wit and Humour, by arising, for the most part from fictitious Contrasts and Coincidences, disqualify the Mind for the Pursuit after Truth, and attending to the useful, practical Relations of Things, as has already been observed in the History of them; and that the State of the Brain which accompanies Mirth cannot subsist long, or return frequently, without injuring it; but must, from the very Frame of our Natures, end at last in the opposite State of Sorrow, Dejection, and Horror. . . . There is [moreover], for the most part, great Vain-glory and Ostentation in all Attempts after Wit and Humour. Men of Wit seek to be admired and caressed by others for the Poignancy, Delicacy, Brilliancy, of their Sayings, Hints, and Repartees; and are perpetually racking their Inventions from this Desire of Applause.[58]

But all this does not mean that the pleasures (and sources of the pleasures) of imagination must be forthwith eradicated; for the pleasures of imagination

> have, in their proper Place and Degree, a great Efficacy in improving and perfecting our Natures. They are to Men in the early Part of their adult Age, what Playthings are to Children; they teach them a Love for Regularity, Exactness, Truth, Simplicity; they lead them to the Knowlege of many important Truths relating to themselves, the external

---

[58] II. 58, p. 252. On the other hand, Hartley staunchly denies that sober, mirthless "Pursuit of Science" is automatic assurance of virtue and piety; for nothing "can easily exceed the Vain-glory, Self-conceit, Arrogance, Emulation, and Envy, that are found in the eminent Professors of the Sciences, Mathematics, Natural Philosophy, and even Divinity itself" (II. 60, p. 255).

World, and its Author; they habituate to invent, and reason
by Analogy and Induction; and when the social, moral, and
religious Affections begin to be generated in us, we may make
a much quicker Progress towards the Perfection of our Natures by having a due Stock, and no more than a due Stock,
of Knowlege in natural and artificial Things, of a Relish
for natural and artificial Beauty. It deserves particular No-
tice here, that the Language used in respect of the Ideas,
Pleasures, and Pains of Imagination, is applicable to those of
the Moral Sense with a peculiar Fitness and Significancy; as,
vice versa, the proper Language of the Moral Sense does, in
many Cases, add great Beauty to Poetry, Oratory, *&c.* when
used catachrestically. And we may observe in general, that as
the Pleasures of Imagination are manifestly intended to gen-
erate and augment the higher Orders, particularly those of
Sympathy, Theopathy, and the Moral Sense; so these last
may be made to improve and perfect those.[59]

And the "actual" treachery in particular of the liberal arts of
poetry, painting, and music as commonly practiced does not
necessitate their complete expulsion from Hartley's associative theocracy.

All these Arts are capable of being devoted to the immediate
Service of God and Religion in an eminent manner; and,
when so devoted, they not only improve and exalt the Mind,
but are themselves improved and exalted to a much higher
Degree, than when employed upon profane Subjects; the
Dignity and Importance of the Ideas and Scenes drawn from
Religion adding a peculiar Force and Lustre thereto. And,

[59] II. 55, pp. 244–45. See also I. 99, p. 496: "The great Suitableness of all
the Virtues to each other, and to the Beauty, Order, and Perfection of
the World, animate and inanimate, impresses a very lovely Character upon
Virtue; and the contrary Self-contradiction, Deformity, and mischievous
Tendency of Vice, render it odious, and Matter of Abhorrence to all
Persons that reflect upon these Things; and beget a Language of this Kind,
which is borrowed, in great measure, from the Pleasures and Pains of
Imagination, and applied with a peculiar Force and Fitness to this Subject
from its great Importance."

upon the Whole, it will follow, that the polite Arts are scarce to be allowed, except when consecrated to religious Purposes; but that here their Cultivation may be made an excellent Means of awakening and alarming our Affections, and transferring them upon their true Objects.[60]

Even mirth and humor—when purified into their proper form of "cheerfulness"—not only are allowable but seem to be requisite.

This [cheerful] Temper of Mind flows from Benevolence and Sociality, and in its Turn begets them; it relieves the Mind, and qualifies us for the Discharge of serious and afflicting Duties, when the Order of Providence lays them upon us; it is a Mark of Uprightness and Indifference to the World, this infantine Gayety of Heart being most observable in those who look upon all that the World offers as mere Toys and Amusements; and it helps to correct, in ourselves and others, many little Follies and Absurdities, which, though they scarce deserve a severer Chastisement, yet ought not to be overlooked intirely.[61]

It is clear, then, that the second of Hartley's discussions of poetry must finally be given general precedence over the first; for he is convinced that all the arts and sciences are more elegant and useful when devoted to God and the welfare of mankind than when pursued with any other motive; that the higher qualities of benevolence, piety, and the moral sense are the only things which "can give a genuine and permanent Lustre" to the philosopher's truths or to the beauties of nature and art; that however perfect a man's intellectual com-

---

[60] II. 59, p. 254.

[61] *Ibid.*, p. 253. And the "Pursuit of Truth" (cf. above, note 58) is an "Entertainment suitable to our rational Natures, and a Duty to him who is the *Fountain of all Knowlege and Truth.*" When it is "entered upon with a View to the Glory of God, and the Good of Mankind, there is no Employment more worthy of our Natures, or more conducive to their Purification and Perfection" (II. 60, pp. 255–56).

prehension of the benevolent and sublime universe of God's creation may be, if he lacks a "Share of the original Source," a real "Love for that boundless Ocean of Love," and a "Sense of Duty to Him," his inquiries and observations are inevitably unsatisfying.[62] The main principles of morality and of the evaluation of the arts which Hartley presents in Part Two derive from religious dogma, not from the "scientific" analysis of the frame and connection of the body and mind in Part One. But the "scientific" analysis in Part One is nevertheless religious in basic import itself in the sense that it both presupposes and reflects the main religious concepts of Part Two. From the very start, it is an analysis of a creature known a priori to be fallen; the mechanism of the human mind is a mark of man's degenerate state, caused by Adam's having eaten the pomel fruit.[63] The unity of Hartley's theory of poetry is found thus in his determination to exert upon the natural phenomena of poetic "behavior" two closely related religious criteria by which those phenomena may be evaluated and regulated. First, although poetry normally partakes of both artificial and natural beauty, its affective power is mainly a mechanical result of exact and just imitation of the affective properties of nature; exact and just imitations can be admitted to some extent into the pious, benevolent, and moral scheme of human life because they will not lie to us too flagrantly about the observable natural world—that world in which we may discern reflections of God and his plan. Second, poetry is therefore potentially useful for promoting piety, benevolence, and morality among men, but only if its natural powers are consecrated to the benevolent purposes and laws of true religion which are made known to man in both natural and scriptural evidences.

The poet is not, however, an inferior philosopher; poets and philosophers are concerned, as Hartley views them, with

---

62 II. 56, pp. 246–48.
63 II. 12, p. 48.

producing different kinds of things, and he argues that
neither poets nor philosophers can have any assurance that
their inventions are not made out of mere shadows of the true
realities. Nevertheless, in the context of God's providence, of
the duty and expectations of mankind, the value of all the
"liberal arts" is below that of the pursuit of "science." It is the
scientists, he is sure, who are "the *Wise, who in the Time of
the End shall understand,* and make an *Increase of Knowlege;* who, by studying, and comparing together, the Word
and Works of God, shall be enabled to illustrate and explain
both; and who, *by turning many to Righteousness, shall* themselves *shine as the Stars for ever and ever." *[64] In a more general sense, the poet, the orator, the historian, and the philosopher or scientist are all required to reach a level of aspiration and devotion which places them in competition, as it
were, with a supreme dialectician and legislator. The competition is inevitably (but properly) uneven, although the su-

---

[64] II. 60, p. 256. It is important to see, of course, that Hartley thinks of
poetry largely in the restricted sense of a depictive art which "by nature"
bears much closer resemblance to history and oratory than to philosophy;
the poetry he speaks of has subject matter which resembles human events
and characters, and he views oratory itself in largely historical rather
than philosophical-didactic terms. The poet's depictions tend to compete
with real history, of which they are imitations; in fact, the poet must
strive to make his fictions appear to be real history. If he had included
philosophical-didactic poems in his initial conception of poetry, perhaps
he would have been urged to apply (at least to such poems) criteria of
philosophical truth as well as of moral value and resemblance to history
and life; or if he had been able to provide man with a positive means of
rising completely in this life to a perception of the highest reality of God,
he perhaps would have been urged to see ordinary human philosophy as
concerned with an "imitation" of that reality in a more direct and specific
sense than he does, and thus to evaluate both poetry and philosophy primarily in terms of their respective ability to "apprehend" the ultimate
reality more or less accurately and properly. Having in the first place
denied man the ability to form an adequate idea (image) of God, Hartley
quite consistently denies the "depictive" artist the dignity of being viewed
as an inferior philosopher—even though the philosopher himself has no
better perceptive idea of God, his supremacy being apparently in his
greater "understanding" of reality.

preme philosopher-king died long ago on a cross; for he died only in human form, and lives on both in spirit and power (as God) and in the scriptural testament by which his life and teachings are revealed to men.[65]

INSPIRATION AND ENTHUSIASM

There is something of a logical difficulty, however, involved in Hartley's portrayal of man in Part One as a "mechanism," determined by his circumstances and by a "necessary" law of association and thus lacking ultimate free will, and his elaboration in Part Two of a highly demanding prescriptive "rule of life" that is to be followed voluntarily. It is not immediately clear how poets, for example, might be capable of conforming to God's will at all as it applies to them, unless their frames and circumstances naturally or normally produce this result; and plainly, in Hartley's view, they do not—which is precisely why the prescriptive rule of life is called for. He was well aware of this difficulty, and in his effort to remove it he does not relinquish the principles of mechanism and necessity, for they are basic to his conception of the fallen condition of man. Instead, he first distinguishes "practical" (common and ordinary) from "philosophical" (ultimate and unlimited) free will, arguing that the doctrine of necessity denies man only the latter, that common voluntary actions, though always finally reducible, like all other human things, to the association of variable experiences, are real and socially indispensable.[66] Since, however, the special actions of men *are* determined mechanically by accidental circumstances, Hartley reasons further that the specific ability to conform to God's will rather than to some other order or pattern cannot be denied without denying also the very possibility of human adherence to true religion; and from this impossible conse-

---

[65] See, e.g., II. 93, p. 407–8.
[66] See Introd. to Part II, pp. 2–3.

quence he moves to the solution that at least some men (and this apparently includes some poets) are given as part of their basic "frame"—in either a natural or a supernatural manner —a special efficiency to exert their common voluntary powers toward conforming to God's will, if the conditioning circumstances include the means of producing awareness of what that will commands.

For Religion being the Regulation of our Affections and Actions according to the Will of God, it presupposes, that after this Will is made known to us, and we, in consequence thereof, become desirous of complying with it, a sufficient Power of complying with it should be put into our Hands. . . . since Religion requires of a Man this Regulation of his Affections and Actions, and since the Powers hitherto mentioned are all grounded upon a sufficient Desire thus to regulate himself, it must presuppose a Power of generating this sufficient Desire, and so on till we come to something which the Man is already possessed of, as Part of his mental Frame, either conferred in a supernatural Way, or acquired in the usual Course of Nature. . . . Religion not only requires and presupposes the common voluntary Powers, by which we perform and forbear Actions, and new-model our Affections, but also whatever else, voluntary or involuntary, is necessary for the actual Exertion of these Powers. And the Connexion between these Points seems to be immediate and undeniable; to require any Thing, must be to require all that is necessary for that Thing. And yet, since all Men do not act up to the Precepts of Religion [i.e., the true religion], it seems undeniable, on the other hand, that some want something that is necessary, immediately or mediately, for the actual Exertion of the proper voluntary Powers over their Affections and Actions. Now, I see no Way of extricating ourselves from this Difficulty, but by supposing, that those who want this one necessary Thing at present, will, however, obtain it hereafter, and that they who shall obtain it at any distant future Time, may be said to have obtained it already, in the Eye of him to whom past, present, and future, are all present, *who quickeneth the Dead, and calleth the Things that be not as though they were.*[67]

Hartley seems to have conceived this "necessary thing" conferred by God not as equivalent either to an "innate idea" or to an "instinct" (both of which he denies to man in general), but as a kind of special dispensation, the need for which is explained by his view of mankind as having fallen from a general state of grace in which all possessed unerring perception of God's will and actively conformed to it. Apparently, then, the practical attempt to turn *all* men in this fallen world toward conforming to the prescriptive rule of life and to apply the "criterion of religion" to all human activities is to be viewed as logically defensible by virtue of the fact that it is God, not man, who decides who has or has not the special grace, and when particular men will or will not conform, in this world. Viewed in this way the rule of life is not a useless speculation but an imperative, both theoretical and practical.

Inasmuch as poets are men, we may infer that the special enabling grace of God can extend to them; but it is not divine inspiration in any of the usual senses. Although Hartley suggests that the "necessary thing" might be "conferred in a supernatural Way," when he comes to discuss the question of divine inspiration as such, he fails to find anything like a special supernatural influence in either ancient heathen or "modern" writers. According to Hartley, men have offered three theories concerning the inspired character of the divine scriptures. He does not wish to decide which of these "approaches nearest to the Truth," [68] but he is certain at least that the first of them is valid—that "all the Passages delivered by *Moses* to the Prophets, as coming from God, and by the Evangelists, as the Words of Christ, also the Revelation given

---

[67] II. 14. 53–55. Cf. *Transactions of the Halifax Antiquarian Society,* 1938, pp. 251–57, 268–69.
[68] II. 19, p. 83.

to St. *John* in a Divine Vision, with all parallel Portions of Scripture, must be considered as divinely inspired, and as having immediate Divine Authority." [69] He believes also in the strength of a second view, that although minor historical and "non-religious" incidents depicted may not have divine authority,

> all the rest of the Scriptures, the Reasoning, the Application of the Prophecies, and even the Doctrines of inferior Note, must be inspired; else what can be meant by the Gifts of the Spirit, particularly that of Prophecy, *i.e.* of instructing others? How can *Christ*'s Promise of the Comforter, who should lead his Disciples into *all Truth,* be fulfilled? Will not the very Essentials of Religion, the Divine Mission of *Christ,* Providence, and a future State, be weakened by thus supposing the sacred Writers to be mistaken in religious Points? And though the History and the Reasonings of the Scriptures have the Marks of being written in the same manner as other Books, *i.e.* may seem not to be inspired, yet a secret Influence might conduct the Writers in every Thing of Moment, even when they did not perceive it, or reflect upon it themselves; it being evident from obvious Reasonings, as well as from the foregoing Theory, that the natural Workings of the Mind are not to be distinguished from [i.e., they appear exactly like] those, which a Being that has a sufficient Power over our intellectual Frame, might excite in us.[70]

He confesses, moreover, that he is even inclined to believe the third view,

> that serious, inquisitive Men . . . will be led by the successive clearing of Difficulties, and unfolding of the most wonderful Truths, to believe the whole Scripture to be inspired, and to abound with numberless Uses and Applications, of which

---

[69] *Ibid.,* pp. 80–81.
[70] *Ibid.,* p. 82.

we yet know nothing. Let future Ages determine. The
evidently miraculous Nature of one Part, *viz.* the proph-
etical, disposes the Mind to believe the Whole to be far
above human Invention, or even Penetration, till such time
as our Understandings shall be farther opened by the Events
which are to precede the second Coming of *Christ.*[71]

These are matters of specific detail which perhaps we shall
never in this life be able to determine, although, in a more
general sense, it is obvious that at least part of the message of
the scriptures derives from divine inspiration.

In such matters of specific detail, where our limited powers
and lowly condition produce only confusion and perplexity,
he recommends a kind of freedom of examination. It is not
for the Shaftesburian reason that this will tend to allow the
final truth to emerge, but rather for the distinctly practical
Christian reason that (given the common understanding that
final truth in such matters is for us impossible) it might tend
to reduce the excessive pride and self-conceit among different
Christian sects and the violent conflicts which arise over just
such unresolvable questions. We should resign ourselves to
humbly and patiently waiting for final illumination. "In the
mean while, let Critics and learned Men of all Kinds have full
Liberty to examine the sacred Books; and let us be sparing in
our Censures of each other. *Let us judge nothing before the
Time, until the Lord come; and then shall every Man have
Praise of God.* Sobriety of Mind, Humility, and Piety, are requisite in the Pursuit of Knowlege of every Kind, and much
more in that of sacred." Then he points out that he has tried to
be impartial toward the three specific theories concerning the
divine inspiration of the scriptures. But he urges that their
advocates *"are all Brethren,* and ought not to *fall out by the
Way,"* and it is clear that he has not questioned for a moment
the "principal fact" of divine inspiration in the scriptures.[72]

---

71 *Ibid.,* p. 83.
72 *Ibid.,* pp. 83–84.

Like most things, however, "inspiration" can be discussed in terms of a real and an unreal, and a higher and a lower, state or form. Thus Hartley distinguishes the claims of the pagan lawgivers to divine inspiration from the real inspiration recorded in the scriptures:

> . . . the Pretences of Lawgivers amongst the Pagans to Inspiration, and the Submission of the People to them, may be accounted for in the Degree in which they are found, from the then Circumstances of Things, without having recourse to real Inspiration; and particularly . . . if we admit the patriarchal Revelations related and intimated by *Moses,* and his own Divine Legation, it will appear, that the Heathen Lawgivers copied after these; which is a strong Argument for admitting them.[73]

Real inspiration can be contrasted also with the "instinct" that governs the lives of brutes, which may be called "a Kind of Inspiration" that mixes itself with and assists "that Part of their Faculties which corresponds to Reason in us, and which is extremely imperfect in them." This kind of inspiration "might be called natural, as proceeding from the same stated Laws of Matter and Motion as the other Phænomena of Nature."[74] Brutes lack the rational powers bestowed on man, especially inasmuch as they lack man's power of language; but they do have certain powers which "are evidently not the Result of external Impressions . . . in the manner according to which . . . the rational Faculties of Mankind are formed and improved; and yet, in the Instances to which they extend, they very much resemble the rational Faculties of Mankind."[75]

The "inspiration" which assists the imperfect faculties of brutes Hartley tends to deny to mankind in general, heathen

---

[73] II. 21, p. 89.
[74] I. 93, p. 412.
[75] *Ibid.,* p. 411.

or otherwise (at least he severely limits its significance); [76] but, in a statement reminiscent of Socrates' criticism of Ion, he observes that animals "much resemble Persons of narrow Capacities and Acquisitions, who yet excel greatly in some particular Art or Science; of which there are many Instances." [77] And these persons are not truly learned; they are limited to a very small portion of knowledge. They show great "Ingenuity in those Things to which they are accustomed, and in some others that border upon them within certain Limits, so as to show great Ingenuity still, though put a little out of their way; but if they be put much out of their way, or questioned about things that are intirely foreign to the Art or Science in which they excel, they are quite lost and confounded." [78] This description of the "ingenious" but highly limited person closely resembles an essential part of Hartley's description of the typical poet or of the "virtuoso" in the liberal arts: "Eminent Votaries of this Kind are generally remarkable for Ignorance and Imprudence in common Affairs; and thus they are exposed to much Ridicule and Contempt, as well as to other great Inconveniences." [79] Their special pursuit, limited though it is, requires a great expenditure of time which prevents them from pursuing the activities necessary for their welfare as men.[80] Hartley does not say, however, that

---

[76] "If we admit the Power of Association, and can also shew that Associations, sufficient in Kind and Degree, concur, in fact, in the several Instances of our intellectual Pleasures and Pains, this will, of itself, exclude all other Causes for these Pleasures and Pains, such as Instinct for Instance. If we cannot trace out Associations sufficient in Kind and Degree, still it will not be necessary to have recourse to other Causes, because great Allowances are to be made for the Novelty, Complexness, and Intricacy of the Subject. However, on the other hand, Analogy may perhaps lead us to conclude, that as Instinct prevails much, and Reason a little, in Brutes, so Instinct ought to prevail a little in us. Let the Facts speak for themselves" (Part I, p. 417).

[77] I. 93, p. 411.

[78] *Ibid.*, pp. 411–12.

[79] II. 55, p. 243.

[80] See e.g., II. 55, pp. 242–44; II. 59, p. 254.

poets are "naturally" or "divinely" inspired, and he goes on finally to contrast the natural brute inspiration with "the Inspiration of the sacred Writers." The latter "appears to be of a much higher Source, so as to be termed supernatural properly, in Contradistinction to all Knowlege resulting from the common Laws of Nature." [81] But (although the argument as a whole suggests that ordinary poets are very much like the lower brutes) it is the brutes that receive the natural inspiration, and the ordinary poets, like other men now in this fallen world, are confined largely to the operations of sensation, memory, imagination—and reason.

The basis of these limitations, of course, is explicitly religious. To claim the privilege of divine inspiration for ordinary poets would be to condone the vice of "enthusiasm," which Hartley defines as "a *mistaken* Persuasion in any Person, that he is a peculiar Favourite with God; and that he receives supernatural Marks thereof." [82] It is a degeneration of the *love* of God.[83] Certain kinds of people tend to have this false belief more than others, and Hartley describes these people in terms much like those which he applies to ordinary poets and poetasters.

> The Vividness of the Ideas of this Class easily generates this false Persuasion in Persons of strong Fancies, little Experience in divine Things, and narrow Understandings (and especially where the Moral Sense, and the Scrupulosity attending its Growth and Improvement, are but imperfectly formed), by giving a Reality and Certainty to all the Reveries of a Man's own Mind, and cementing the Associations in a preternatural Manner. It may also be easily contracted by Contagion, as daily Experience shews; and indeed more easily than most other Dispositions from the glaring Language used by Enthusiasts, and from the great Flattery and

---

81 I. 93, p. 412.
82 I. 98, p. 490; italics added. See I. 95, p. 437.
83 I. 98, p. 488.

Support, which Enthusiasm affords to Pride and Self-conceit.[84]

And yet, again, he does not discuss this enthusiastic tendency in relation particularly to poets and poetry. He is convinced that most kinds of poetry, painting, and music, especially the ancient heathen and the modern patterned after it, "cannot be enjoyed without *evil Communications,* and Concurrence in the Pagan Shew and Pomp of the World," and the proof of such evil communications can be observed by anyone with "a duly serious Frame of Mind" in public Diversions, Collections of Pictures, Academies for Painting, Statuary, &c. antient heathen Poetry, modern Poetry of most Kinds, Plays, Romances, &c." [85] But he does not associate these dangerous and sinful institutions and their evil contagion specifically with a false belief in the special favor of God. Nor—in spite of a few scattered references to both good and evil spirits (discovering the nature of which is a task given to religion) [86]—does he make a connection between the evil communications of most poetry and the actual direct influence of demons or of Satan himself. The question is simply not raised. This is potentially consistent, of course, with his view of the fallen condition of man; for to grant poets direct and positive contact with evil spiritual beings would perhaps lay the basis for such contact in this world with good spirits also. In Hartley's derogatory definition of "enthusiasm" the etymology of the word has no positive significance; and it is not possible (as it is for many of his other concepts) to view "enthusiasm" in both a real and an unreal, or a better and a worse, form or state. The dialectical opposition here is between enthusiasm (unreal) and the divine inspiration of the scriptures (real). Thus, a poet might

---

84 *Ibid.,* pp. 490–91.
85 I. 59, p. 254. Cf. II. 53, pp. 236–38; II. 14, p. 53.
86 See I. 88, p. 354.

well be an "enthusiast"; but no divine spirits, either good or evil, are controlling his production on that account.

THE IMITATION OF GOD

The evil communications of ordinary poetry, then, apparently must be attributed simply to the inherent falsity and immorality of the subject matter which, as the invented product of a fallen creature, it normally presents; and if a poet is able to avoid such evil communications it is because he can regulate his inventions according to the precepts of true religion, not because God is directing him or supplying the substance in any special inspirational way. Although it is more than probable that all human mental operations and ideas are ultimately *caused* by God, it is not clear whether the mind is material or spiritual; the exact manner in which God operates is beyond man's powers to determine. Even if we suppose the human soul to be immaterial (as Hartley tends to favor doing), still all our sensations and ideas are *connected* directly and reciprocally with movements of the body and of external objects; not only is the exact character of God's efficient relation to these movements a mystery, but whether God works in general through the spiritual or the material part of the human frame is also uncertain. Hence it is impossible for a poet, or anyone else, to verify any notion of a special communication from God. Hartley thus denies the divine "authority" of all written documents but the holy scriptures.

Nor can any inference be drawn from the resemblance between the scriptures and the productions of common poets. He notes that the scriptures contain much figurative language, and that the "imaginative" process by which in part both poems and dreams are made resembles the process operating particularly in the prophecies, which are unquestionably the creations of God himself, not of man. But it is not the figurativeness as such of the scriptures as a whole which determines their "genuineness" and divine authority,[87] and the connections among imagination, dreams, and prophecies remain those of a limited and imperfect analogy. Prophecies, like dreams and poems,

> deal chiefly in visible Imagery; they abound with apparent Impossibilities, and Deviations from common Life, of which yet the Prophets take not the least Notice: They speak of new Things as of familiar ones; they are carried in the Spirit from Place to Place; Things requiring a long Series of Time in real Life, are transacted in the prophetical Visions, as soon as seen; they ascribe to themselves and others new Names, Offices, &c.; every Thing has a real Existence conferred upon it; there are singular Combinations of Fragments of visible Appearances; and God himself is represented in a visible Shape, which of all Things must be most offensive to a pious *Jew*.[88]

Although this resemblance to imagination and dreaming is somehow good evidence of "the Genuineness of the Prophecies, exclusively of all other Evidences," [89] he does not go on to conclude that the productions of poets might also on this basis be "genuine" in their relation to God. Even if poets dealt exclusively with the proper religious subjects we apparently could not draw such an inference; the divine scriptures have already been written.

It is not difficult, then, to explain Hartley's failure to adopt the conception, so important to Shaftesbury and Akenside, of the poet as a successful imitator of divine creativity. The poet, as poet, imitates the product of God's creativity, but not the act of divine creation. Hartley in fact denies man the ability to form a "just Idea" of God's own creative process, in terms of which we might describe the poet's analogous process. He

---

87 See II. 22, pp. 97–98; II. 26, pp. 126–36.
88 I. 91, p. 389.
89 *Ibid*. Cf. II. 22, pp. 97–98.

does, however, list God's attributes, in general terms, and it quickly becomes clear that in his view the poet's powers of invention are nothing approaching or resembling the great powers and qualities possessed by God; and, of course, without some indication that human mental processes are not resolvable into the mechanical operations of association, it would be ridiculous to think of poets as at all "creative." God is infinite in power, knowledge, and goodness. He is the first cause of everything, unlimited, and eternal. He is also capable of "Creations in Time . . . of Things made from nothing." [90] Human invention, in contrast, is a combination of memory, imagination, and the habit of forming and pursuing analogies, all of which are "reconcileable with, and deducible from, the Power of Association, and the Mechanism of the Mind." In other words, God is an infinitely independent and free being, capable of creation in the strictest, highest, and most absolute sense, whereas the human poet is a finite, dependent, and captive being, capable, at best, only of *reorganizing* acquired and associated impressions and images into complex thoughts which, as such, have not been expressed in prior literary models.[91] The poet is dependent upon prior associations not only for the materials with which he works but for the structure which he attempts to give these materials. The human inventive ability can be called a "power" only in a limited and secondary sense; [92] "all the Actions of Man proceed ultimately from God, the one universal Cause." [93]

Moreover, the poet who lacks a proper devotion to the will of God, to the motives, subjects, beauties, and perfections of religion, not only is responsible for "evil communications"

90 II. 3, p. 12.
91 I. 94, pp. 434–35.
92 See, e.g., II. 16, pp. 66–70.
93 II. 15, p. 61.

wholly opposed to the laws and admonishments of God, but
also, by the agency of this deviation and corruption, is actually *destructive* of the proper moral order, rather than "creative" in any sense. Such a poet is engaged, though perhaps
unwittingly, in the satanic activity of opposing God's creation.
Much as "the Idolatry of the Heathens, and their Ignorance
of the true God, must have produced an utter Perversion and
Corruption of their moral Sense," the reading of "lewd
heathen Poets, modern Plays, &c.," which are so corrupt in
the pleasures of sensation, in temptations, and destitute of
religious motives, inevitably produces immediate "destructive
consequences" which cannot be "balanced" by any other
worldly considerations.[94] The inventions and expressions of
the ordinary unredeemed poet may be viewed thus as opposed
to that aspect of divine "creativity" which relates to man's
making of himself what is possible and proper according to
God's infinitely benevolent providence. No man, of course,
could be judged capable of actually thwarting the fulfillment
of God's providential design, but the common poet stands,
nevertheless, as one of the main symbols of the satanic opposition to God's will that has characterized human life since the
beguilement of Adam and Eve.

There is, however, an important, though restricted, sense in
which Hartley does speak positively of the "imitation" of the
deity. Although God is the only true creator, both as original
maker and as final maintainer and father, man *is* able to imitate the creativity of God by "concurring" with His plan for
the welfare of all His creatures, rather than with the pagan
show and pomp of the world. And in this context Hartley
tends to bring together the concepts of human knowledge of
the true attributes of God, inspiration (though in a rather
loose sense), and divine creativity, in relation to man's fundamental task of obeying the *will* of God.

---

[94] II. 12, p. 48. Cf. II. 53, p. 238.

Now it is at once evident, that the Consideration of the infinite Power, Knowlege, and Goodness of God, of his Holiness, Justice, Veracity, and Mercy, and of his being our Creator, Governor, Judge, and Father, must inspire us with that Tendency to comply with his Will, which, according to the proper Use of Language, is called a Sense of *Duty, Obligation,* of what we *ought* to do. It is evident also, that the Will of God must be determined by his Attributes and Appellations. He must therefore will, that we should apply to him, as we do to earthly Superiors of the same Character, purifying, however, and exalting our Affections to the utmost; that we should be merciful, holy, just, *&c.* in Imitation of him, and because this is to concur with him in his great Design of making all his Creatures happy; and lastly, that we should so use the Pleasures of Sense, and the Enjoyments of this World, as not to hurt ourselves or others.[95]

Hartley argues that compliance with the moral sense, the sum and culmination of all the intellectual pleasures, is a man's primary means of obedience to the will of God, of constructively ordering his life and actions in harmony with the supreme plan for mankind's present and future existence.[96] And there is no reason why this cannot particularly be the aim and hope of those men called poets, whose special "imitative" inventions, and figurative and rhythmic expressions, although generally inferior to the works of the scientist, may be eminently useful to awaken and direct the affections and actions of other men—if their subjects are determined by the precepts of religion, and not by the example of ancient heathen models or by uncontrolled copying of the ruins of our first paradise. The poet's constructive "power," according to the true scheme of things, is thus finally a matter of the way in which his behavior as a maker of affective structures of

[95] II. 12, pp. 46–47.
[96] *Ibid.*, p. 47.

"fiction" may be controlled by his moral conduct as a man. And God has been provident:

> . . . lest the best of Men, in considering the Number and Greatness of their Sins, and comparing them with the Purity of the Scripture-Precepts, and the Perfection of God, should not dare to look up to him with a filial Trust and Confidence in him, lest their Hearts should fail, Christ our Saviour is sent from Heaven, God manifest in the Flesh, that whosoever believeth in him should not perish, but have everlasting Life; that, though our Sins be as Scarlet, they should by him, by means of his Sufferings, and our Faith, be made as white as Wool; and the great Punishment, which must otherwise have been inflicted upon us according to what we call the Course of Nature, be averted. Faith then in Christ the Righteous will supply the Place of that Righteousness, and sinless Perfection, to which we cannot attain.[97]

---

[97] II. 93, pp. 407–8.

⧼ 5 ⧽

Harris and the Dialectic
of Books

JAMES HARRIS OF SALISBURY DEVOTED HIS INTELLECTUAL
life to the task of stimulating interest in philosophical and
literary treasures, especially those of ancient Greece and
Rome. His chief purposes as a writer, he declared, were "to
enlarge the bounds of science; to revive the decaying taste of
antient literature; to lessen the bigotted contempt of everything not modern; and to assert to authors of every age their
just portion of esteem." [1] Although he was apparently quite

---

[1] *Hermes: Or a Philosophical Inquiry Concerning Universal Grammar,* 5th
ed. (London, 1794), Preface, p. xv. I have modified Harris' rather osten-
tatious typography in all quotations, retaining only initial capitals on
some especially important terms. The *Hermes,* Harris' most famous work,
was first published in 1751. *Three Treatises: The First Concerning Art,
the Second Concerning Music, Painting, and Poetry, the Third Concerning Happiness* was first published in 1744; the 4th edition (London, 1783)
is used here. *Philosophical Arrangements* is used in the 1st edition (London,
1775). *Philological Inquiries, in Three Parts* is also used in the 1st edition
(London, 1781).
　Harris' writings, though little studied in recent times, were read and
cited by important authors during and after his life, and the *Three
Treatises* and *Hermes* enjoyed popularity enough to be printed in a number of eighteenth-century editions. Although it cannot be said that he was
one of the period's great and original intellectual figures, as one of a
number of interesting minor writers who rebelled against the traditions
of empiricism, materialism, and psychologistic analysis in the second half
of the century he perhaps deserves somewhat more extensive study than
he has been given by recent scholars. The *Hermes* has been examined by
Otto Funke, in *Studien zur Geschichte der Sprachphilosophie* (Bern, 1927),
pp. 5–48, and in *Englische Sprachphilosophie im späteren 18. Jahrhundert*

well read in modern philosophy, criticism, and poetry, and able to find value in them when it was there to be found, he remained unimpressed, throughout his career, by the claims of modern associationists and psychological relativists (and in general of most empirical analysts of the pleasures of imagination and taste) that they had finally put matters of art and letters on a solid scientific basis. Dr. Johnson's remark that Harris did not understand his own "system" was probably not wholly unjustified, though a more recent assertion that Harris approaches "lunacy" is perhaps too strong.[2] If it would be rash to claim for him either philosophical profundity or complete consistency among his various works, it can at least be said that he possessed a broad awareness of the ancient origins and analogues of many of the principles and doctrines presented to the world in his time as fresh and modern; and his controlling intention, after all, was more scholarly and pedagogical than philosophical—it was to "excite (if possible) the curiosity of readers, to examine with stricter attention those valuable remains of antient literature."[3]

But Harris was not a mere antiquary, nor only a historian; he was an exhibitor and organizer of the unappreciated writings of men, and this helps to justify, at least to him, the seeming pedantry of his including in his works so many extracts from both ancient and modern poets and philosophers:

> It was not from an ostentatious wish to fill his page with quotations, that the author has made such frequent and cop-

---

(Bern, 1934), pp. 8–21 and *passim*. Some aspects of the influence of Harris' work (especially the *Three Treatises*) in Germany are surveyed in G. J. ten Hoor, *James Harris and the Influence of his Aesthetic Theories in Germany* (Unpublished dissertation, University of Michigan, 1929). See also H. von Stein, *Die Entstehung der neueren Ästhetik* (Stuttgart, 1886).

2 See Boswell's *Life of Johnson, Aetat.* 69 (ed. R. W. Chapman [Oxford, 1953], p. 911); George Boas, *The Limits of Reason* (New York, 1961), p. 97. Johnson would seem to be referring here to the "system" of Harris' *Philosophical Arrangements*, whereas Boas probably has in mind the *Hermes.*

3 *Thr. Tr.*, p. 249.

ious extracts from other authors. . . . From the writers al-
leged, both ancient and modern, the reader will perceive,
how important and respectable these authorities are. He will
perceive too, that, in the wide regions of Being, some sages
having cultivated one part, and some another, the labours of
ancients and moderns have been often different, when not
hostile; often various,, when not contradictory; and that,
among the valuable discoveries of later periods, there are
many so far from clashing with the ancient doctrines here
advanced, that they coincide as amicably, as a Chillingworth
and an Addison in the same library; a Raphael and Claude
in the same gallery.[4]

Behind this practical desire, moreover, there is a general metaphysical rationale, offering both an immediate justification
for antiquarian studies and a special theory of truth and of
philosophical method. For example, when he is concentrating
his attention on the "liberal arts," Harris' problem is to "establish an important union; the union he means between
taste and truth." Indeed, taste is

but a species of inferior truth. 'Tis the truth of elements, of
decoration, and of grace; which, as all truth is similar and
congenial, co-incides as it were spontaneously with the more
severe and logical; but which, whenever destitute of that
more solid support, resembles some fair but languid body;
a body, specious in feature, but deficient as to nerve; a body,
where we seek in vain for that natural and just perfection,
which arises from that pleasing harmony of strength and
beauty associated.[5]

It was such a "splendid union" of taste and truth "which produced the classics of pure antiquity; which produced . . . the
classics of modern days; and which those, who now write,

---

[4] *Phil. Arr.* XVIII, p. 455–56.
[5] *Ibid.,* pp. 459–60.

ought to cultivate with attention, if they have a wish to survive in the estimation of posterity." [6]

In Harris' conception, however, human art, conduct, and knowledge cannot clearly be separated (or given wholly independent criteria), and the significance of his critical exhibition of the works of other authors goes beyond the task of improving "taste" according to the one universal truth; it includes that of improving "understanding" and the standards of estimating men as well:

> . . . as the authors, whom he has quoted, lived in various ages, and in distant countries; some in the full maturity of Grecian and Roman literature; some in its declension; and others in periods still more barbarous, and depraved; it may afford perhaps no unpleasing speculation, to see how the same Reason has at all times prevailed; how there is one Truth, like one sun, that has enlightened human intelligence through every age, and saved it from the darkness both of sophistry and error.
>
> Nothing can more tend to enlarge the mind, than these extensive views of men, and human knowledge; nothing can more effectually take us off from the foolish admiration of what is immediately before our eyes, and help us to a juster estimate both of present men, and present literature.[7]

It is clear that he is not arguing here merely that certain ancient doctrines happen to be true in spite of their age; he is engaged in determining and illustrating the one truth that has enlightened man from the beginning of his intellectual life. Ultimately he locates it in a "Providential Circulation, which never ceases for a moment thro' every part of the universe," [8] a system of "Exemplars, Patterns, Forms, Ideas (call them as you please)" which emanates from the divine mind.[9]

---

6 *Ibid.*, p. 459. *Cf. Phil. Inq.* II. xii, pp. 223–25.
7 Preface to *Herm.*, pp. x–xi.
8 *Phil. Inq.* III. xv, p. 540.
9 *Herm.* III. iv. 2, p. 380.

The exemplars or forms are the basis of the reality of natural substances and their attributes, and they govern both universal grammar and the simple terms of logic, which are "words representing things, through the medium of our ideas." [10] The scholar-philosopher must apprehend the elements and order of the providential circulation not only in the external and "internal" (mental) parts of nature but also (and perhaps more importantly) in the writings of men; and this process of apprehension may be called a kind of "remembering." [11] The concrete things of nature are not merely embodiments or actualizations but are "copies" or "pictures" of the eternal ideas; nature *reflects* the providential circulation. The divine ideas thus are general a priori patterns of particular things. Human ideas, on the other hand, are both particular and general, and words are the "symbols" of human ideas. The "matter" of language is recognized "when it is considered as a voice"; its "form" is recognized when it is seen to be, through human compact, "significant of our several ideas." [12] Statements in words are true when they are significant of human ideas which correspond, directly or indirectly, to the true eternal intellectual forms of reality that make up the providential circulation.[13]

The capacity to apprehend—or "remember"—these intellectual forms is innate in man, and the various atomist and sensationist explanations of human ideas are all untenable. In these atheistic accounts of things, first comes

> that huge body the sensible world. Then this and its attributes beget sensible ideas. Then out of sensible ideas, by a

---

10 *Phil. Arr.* I, p. 15.

11 For support of this conception Harris goes not only to Plato's *Phaedo* and *Meno* and the various commentaries on them, but also to the Bible, Milton, Epictetus, Marcus Aurelius, and Virgil, among others; see *Herm.* III. iv–v, pp. 401–5n. and *Phil. Inq.* III. xv, pp. 539–42.

12 *Herm.* III. iii, p. 348–49. Cf. *Thr. Tr. II.* iii. 1, p. 70.

13 *Herm.* III. iv. 2, pp. 379–91.

kind of lopping and pruning, are made ideas intelligible, whether specific or general. Thus should they admit that Mind was coeval with Body, yet till Body gave it ideas, and awakened its dormant powers, it could at best have been nothing more, than a sort of dead capacity; for innate ideas it could not possibly have any.

At another time we hear of bodies so exceedingly fine, that their very exility makes them susceptible of sensation and knowledge; as if they shrunk into intellect by their exquisite subtlety, which rendered them too delicate to be bodies any longer. It is to this notion we owe many curious inventions, such as subtle æther, animal spirits, nervous ducts, vibrations, and the like; terms, which modern philosophy, upon parting with occult qualities, has found expedient to provide itself, to supply their place.[14]

But in the "intellectual" scheme, which "never forgets deity," the origin of intelligible ideas, even those in human capacities, is sought in the "primary mental cause," to which everything corporeal is "postponed."

For tho' sensible objects may be the destined medium, to awaken the dormant energies of man's understanding, yet are those energies themselves no more contained in sense, than the explosion of a cannon, in the spark which gave it fire.

In short, all minds, that are, are similar and congenial; and so too are their ideas, or intelligible forms. Were it otherwise, there could be no intercourse between man and man, or (what is more important) between man and God.[15]

Although Harris thus never doubts the superiority of this "intellectual scheme" over its rival system, the characteristic feature of his method is his practice of finding and demonstrating the pervasive truth and influence of the intellectual scheme by means of a kind of scholarly synthesis, in which a

---

14 *Ibid.* III. iv. 3, pp. 392–93.
15 *Ibid.,* pp. 393–97.

great variety of ostensibly different and conflicting philosophies and doctrines are brought into harmony. It is, as it were, a dialectic of great books, governed by a process of perceiving analogies and harmonies among diverse things in a framework of better-worse oppositions and of a large "providential" ontological-historical system. The task is to perceive the "congeniality" among various manifestations of the human mind, the one in the many and diverse. All truth is the same, for all minds are congenial and all languages participate in the universal grammar of eternal ideas.[16]

The mind and language of the ancient Greeks, however, are superior to all others.[17] The genius of the Greek language was its "propriety and universality . . . for all that is great, and all that is beautiful, in every subject, and under every form of writing."[18] It was, that is, unlimited, for the ideas of the Greeks were unlimited; they were not confined to or excessively dominated by particular sciences or partial views of things. Real truth, "having the most intimate connection with the Supreme Intelligence, may be said (as it were) to shine with unchangeable splendor, enlightening throughout the universe every possible subject, by nature susceptible of its benign influence."[19] Deviations from this one, entire truth are caused not only by partial views of things, but also by the imperfections of sense, by idleness, by the "turbulence" of passions, by unfortunate education, and local sentiments, opinions, and beliefs; all these "conspire in many instances to furnish us with ideas, some too general, some too partial, and (what is worse than all this) with many that are erroneous, and contrary to truth."[20] Since in the Greeks Harris finds one of the wisest of nations, where there were many geniuses de-

---

16 See *ibid.* III. v, pp. 403–8.
17 *Ibid.,* pp. 415–24.
18 *Ibid.,* pp. 423–24.
19 *Ibid.,* pp. 403–4.
20 *Ibid.,* p. 406.

void of these common obstacles to the apprehension of original and complete truth, it is fitting that Greek writers should dominate his scholarly program of perceiving and setting forth the eternal forms of truth. But he is not required to ignore the scattered elements of truth which he can find elsewhere and bring into harmony with the whole. To limit his inquiries to the Greeks would cause him to suffer the consequences of partiality himself, and Harris therefore draws readily upon Roman literature and the Bible, as well as upon other writings, European and non-European.[21]

Nor is he unable to perceive differences and conflicts, and their importance, even among the Greeks. But truth is a unity and wholeness of parts; truth is one, and the human mind is essentially one. Consequently, among the diverse theories of men it is possible to abstract, a priori, the basic universals, and to integrate them into one coherent system. And he is prepared to find the "circulation" of that system even among writers who overtly expressed doctrines opposed to it; though ignorant of its operation, such writers may actually participate in the divine circulation, inadvertently expressing its laws and patterns. Thus, for example, he is able to call repeatedly upon Aristotle (who was decidedly critical of Plato's theory of "Ideas") and Democritus (who completely reversed the Platonic system and found true being in atoms and saw all knowledge as derived from sensation). Aristotle's ten categories are, in fact, the chief subject of Harris' *Philosophical Arrangements;* and in his treatment, with the aid of Neoplatonist commentaries,[22] they not only are the simple and general prior forms—the genera—of all human knowledge, but

---

21 See, e.g., *ibid.* III. iv–v, pp. 401–5; *Phil. Arr.* III, p. 43; VI, pp. 100–101, 121–31; see in general his history of criticism and taste in Parts I and III of *Phil. Inq.*, and especially the appendix (pp. 543–71) containing accounts of the Arabic manuscripts and the manuscripts of Livy in the Escurial Library in Spain, the manuscripts of Cebes in the library of the King of France in Paris, and the literature of Russia.

22 See *Herm.* III. iv. 2, pp. 381–88n., for one of the clearest illustrations of this process.

become identified with the true structure of being, the eternal intellectual forms emanating from the mind of God.[23] It does not matter that Aristotle might not have approved; for he was only one of the ancient writers who somehow perceived these universal "forms previous," and (although, in Harris' view, Aristotle was actually a systematizer of Plato's philosophy) he need not have been at all in control of his participation in the providential scheme. In a similar way, Democritus participates in the divine order of ideas in his very expression of the atheistic doctrine of the atoms and the void; for he presents the atoms and the void as *contraries*—Harris having found contrariety to be a universal principle of generation and being (under the genus of *substance*)—and he operates under the genus of *position* in his explanation of the ways in which the least elements acquire complex shapes![24]

Since the eternal intellectual truth is recorded most universally in language and writing, it must be sought principally in the examples of language and writing which have survived from age to age and nation to nation; and man's natural capacities of taste and understanding must be instructed and developed primarily by means of the culture of books.

> And as to those who tell us, with an air of seeming wisdom, that it is men, and not books, we must study to become knowing; this I have always remarked, from repeated experience, to be the common consolation and language of dunces. They shelter their ignorance under a few bright examples, whose transcendent abilities, without the common helps, have been sufficient of themselves to great and important ends. But alas!
>
> *Decipit exemplar vitiis imitabile—*

---

23 See esp. *ibid.*, pp. 382–86; *Phil. Arr.* II, pp. 34–35; XIII, pp. 345–46; XVIII, pp. 454–55, 460–64.

24 See *Phil. Arr.* III, pp. 42–62, esp. p. 44n.; XIII, pp. 339–40, 343–44; cf. *Phil. Inq.* II. i, pp. 50–57.

In truth, each man's understanding, when ripened and mature, is a composite of natural capacity, and of super-induced habit. Hence the greatest men will be necessarily those, who possess the best capacities, cultivated with the best habits. Hence also moderate capacities, when adorned with valuable science, will far transcend others the most acute by nature, when either neglected, or applied to low and base purposes. And thus for the honour of culture and good learning, they are able to render a man, if he will take the pains, intrinsically more excellent than his natural superiors.[25]

The cultivation of a man's "natural capacity" through the study of the enduring writings of men is actually the primary practical means by which the eternal forms are to be "remembered." At the close of his history of medieval letters, criticism, taste, and philosophy which forms the third part of *Philological Inquiries,* Harris fuses the doctrine of reminiscence with a doctrine of historical recurrence which he attributes to the wise man of Ecclesiastes, and argues that ignorance of what has been done in the past is a kind of "forgetfulness"; what is near us in time erroneously appears more important or more striking, because it appears novel, but as the wise man, attempting to save us from these errors, has informed us:

The thing, that hath been, is that, which shall be; and there is no new thing under the sun. Is there any thing whereof it may be said, see, this is new? It hath been already of old time, which was before us.—He then [continues Harris] subjoins the cause of this apparent novelty—things past, when they return, appear new, if they are forgotten; and things present will appear so, should they too be forgotten, when they return.

This forgetfulness of what is similar in events which return (for in every returning event such similarity exists) is

─────────────
[25] *Herm.* III. v, pp. 425–26.

the forgetfulness of a mind uninstructed and weak; a mind ignorant of that great, that Providential Circulation, which never ceases for a moment thro' every part of the universe.

It is not like that forgetfulness, which I once remember in a man of letters, who, when at the conclusion of a long life, he found his memory began to fail, said chearfully—"Now I shall have a pleasure, I could not have before; that of reading my old books, and finding them all new."

There was in this consolation something philosophical and pleasing. And yet perhaps 'tis a higher philosophy (could we attain it) not to forget the past; but in contemplation of the past to view the future, so that we may say on the worst prospects, with a becoming resignation, what Eneas said of old to the Cumean prophetess,

> ——Virgin, no scenes of Ill
> To me or new, or unexpected rise;
> I've seen 'em all; have seen, and long before
> Within myself revolv'd 'em in my mind.

In such a conduct, if well founded, there is not only fortitude, but piety: fortitude, which never sinks, from a conscious integrity; and piety, which never resists, by referring all to the Divine Will.[26]

POETRY AS THE MASTER SCIENCE

Harris' over-all scheme is thus one in which a special dialectical theory of truth and history informs the eclectic activities of a pious scholar devoted to improving the taste and understanding of his fellow men. Within this broad framework, however, he developed specific accounts of the nature and value of poetry which can be viewed in terms of actual doctrine as well as of the various antiquities by which they are supported. In the second of his *Three Treatises,* he offered his contribution to the general discussion, which occupied

---

[26] *Phil. Inq.* III. xv, pp. 539–42. The biblical reference is to Ecclesiastes 7:10; 1:9; 2:16. The reference to Virgil is to the *Aeneid* VI. 103–5.

many of his contemporaries, of the "Aristotelian" problem of the nature of imitation and the relations among the "liberal arts." Painting, music, and poetry, he argues, may be distinguished by their media, but they are all mimetic and share a common end: accurate "representation" or "expression" of reality; hence they may be initially evaluated in relation to their comparative ability to achieve this end, and then (on the basis of the peculiarities of subject matter imposed upon them by the natural limits of their media) in relation to the intrinsic value of the subjects which they best imitate.[27]

The "fittest" subjects for the imitation of painting are such "things" and "incidents" as are "peculiarly characterized by figure and colour." Harris lists ten kinds: (1) things inanimate and vegetable, (2) animal figures, (3) the motions and sounds "peculiar to each animal species, when accompanied with configurations, which are obvious and remarkable," (4) the human body, in its various appearances and positions, (5) the "natural sounds peculiar to the human species," when, as for the sounds of animals, accompanied by visible configurations, (6) all "energies, passions, and affections of the soul, being in any degree more intense or violent than ordinary" that produce "visible effects on the body," (7) "all actions and events, whose integrity or wholeness depends upon a short and self-evident succession of incidents" ("of necessity every picture is a *punctum temporis* or instant"), (8) extended actions whose visible incidents are all similar and congenial, (9) all actions concurring in the same point of time, (10) all actions "which are known, and known universally, rather than actions newly invented or known but to a few."[28]

The inclusion of auditory and "moving" subjects in painting is based on the spectator's intermediate *inference* of sound and motion from the still and visual configurations, positions, and arrangements associable with them, but "things and inci-

---

[27] *Thr. Tr. II.* i. 2–3, pp. 55–59.
[28] *Ibid.* ii. 1, pp. 61–64.

dents, as are most eminently characterized by motion and sound" are the "fittest subjects" for musical imitation.[29] In the inanimate world, "music may imitate the glidings, murmurings, tossings, roarings, and other accidents of water, as perceived in fountains, cataracts, rivers, seas, &c.," and also those similar sounds of thunder and of winds; in the animal world, "it may imitate the voice of some animals, but chiefly that of singing birds"; it may also "faintly copy some of their motions"; in "the human kind, it can also imitate some motions and sounds," especially—most perfectly—those "expressive of grief and anguish."[30] The main power of music does not lie, however, in its imitative abilities, but in its ability to *raise* the passions and affections, and "there is a reciprocal operation between our affections, and our ideas; so that, by a sort of natural sympathy, certain ideas necessarily tend to raise in us certain affections; and those affections, by a sort of counter operation, to raise the same ideas."[31]

Painting is superior, as imitation, to music, but poetry is superior to both painting and music, especially when it is combined with the affective power of music.[32] Poetry imitates in two ways: "naturally," when there is a physical resemblance between the sounds of its medium and the sounds of nature, and "artificially," since its medium is words, "and words are the symbols by compact of all ideas." As natural imitation, poetry is inferior to painting, but roughly equal to music.[33] It is as imitation "by sound significant," however, that poetry obtains its "genuine force." Because poetry "is able to find sounds expressive of every idea, so is there no subject either of picture-imitation, or musical, to which it does not aspire; all things and incidents whatever being, in a manner, to be

---

29 *Ibid.* ii. 2, pp. 65–66.
30 *Ibid.*, pp. 66–67.
31 *Ibid.* vi. 1, p. 96.
32 *Ibid.* ii. 3, pp. 67–69. See also vi. 1, pp. 95, 97–102.
33 *Ibid.* iii. 1–3, pp. 70–74.

described by words." [34] But poetry is inferior to painting "in all subjects [that is, the visible], where painting can fully exert itself"; [35] whereas, in general, music is inferior to poetry, since the sounds of music can raise only similar ideas of natural sounds and motions, while poetry, with its more flexible and expressive medium, can raise the same ideas, and thus "even in subjects the best adapted to musical imitation, the imitation of poetry will be still more excellent." [36] Poetry is best adapted, however, to subjects not really suited to painting or music: (1) all actions "whose whole is of so lengthened a duration, that no point of time, in any part of that whole, can be given fit for painting," and (2) "all subjects so framed, as to lay open the internal constitution of man, and give us an insight into characters, manners, passions, and sentiments." [37]

But the superiority of poetry in general over painting and music lies in the superior merit of these subjects: "They must necessarily of all be the most affecting; the most improving; and such of which the mind has the strongest comprehension." [38] And it soon becomes obvious that in Harris' scheme the great value of poetry turns on its being best adaptable to metaphysical and moral ends, to the problem of teaching man something about himself.

> As to improvement—there can be none surely (to men at least) so great, as that which is derived from a just and decent representation of human manners and sentiments. For what can more contribute to give us that master-knowledge, without which, all other knowledge will prove of little or no utility?
>
> As to our comprehension—there is nothing certainly, of which we have so strong ideas, as of that which happens in

---

34 *Ibid.* iv. 1, pp. 75–76.
35 *Ibid.* iv. 2, p. 79.
36 *Ibid.* iv. 3, p. 81.
37 *Ibid.* v. 2, pp. 83–84.
38 *Ibid.*, p. 85.

the moral or human world. For as to the internal part, or active principle of the vegetable, we know it but obscurely; because there we can discover neither passion, nor sensation. In the animal world indeed this principle is more seen, and that from the passions and sensations which there declare themselves. Yet all still rests upon the mere evidence of sense; upon the force only of external and unassisted experience. But in the moral or human world, as we have a medium of knowledge far more accurate than this; so from hence it is, that we can comprehend accordingly.

With regard therefore to the various events which happen here [in the moral world], and the various causes, by which they are produced—in other words, of all characters, manners, human passions, and sentiments; besides the evidence of sense, we have the highest evidence additional, in having an express consciousness of something similar within; of something homogeneous in the recesses of our own minds; in that, which constitutes to each of us his true and real self.[39]

The conclusion is that poetry is "much superior to either of the other mimetic arts; it having been shewn to be equally excellent in the accuracy of its imitation; and to imitate subjects, which far surpass, as well in utility, as in dignity." [40] And besides acquiring its greater dignity, in a general sense, from its ability to deal with greater and nobler subjects, it obtains a "moral science from the contemplation of human life; an end common both to epic, tragic, and comic poetry." [41]

---

[39] *Ibid.*, pp. 86–89.

[40] *Ibid.* v. 5, p. 94.

[41] *Ibid.* v. 2, p. 86n. Harris adds that "there is a peculiar end to tragedy, that of eradicating the passions of pity and fear." His interpretation of this "Aristotelian" doctrine turns on a supposition of the inferiority and ignobility of these emotions, and he notes that there are none "so devoid of these two passions, as those perpetually conversant, where the occasions of them are most frequent; such, for instance, as the military men, the professors of medicine, chirurgery, and the like." From this "intercourse" their minds grow, as it were, callous; they gain "an apathy by experience,

Poetry offers a useful means of contemplating human life in the quasi-Aristotelian sense that it can present universal forms, not merely particular or historical facts.[42] But Harris adopts a decidedly un-Aristotelian conception of the nature of such forms; the good poet, in his view, presents forms of life which correspond to the true, a priori, inner patterns of human thought, action, and feeling. In other words, these universal forms are not merely generalizations from observed particulars of life (though they may incidentally be this too); they are innate ideas according to which particulars can be shaped in the proper fashion and on the basis of which all human beings may respond and properly cultivate the true inner nature of themselves—may acquire that γνῶσιν ἑαυτῶν which is the "master-science." Rational man, Harris asserts, possesses a "transcendent faculty, by which he is made conscious not only of what . . . [his mind] feels, but of the powers themselves, which are the sources of those very feelings; a faculty, which recognizing both itself and all things else, becomes a canon, a corrector, and a standard universal." And to rational minds alone "is imparted that Master-Science, of what they are, where they are, and the end to which they are destined."[43] In its most fully and properly developed form, this "master-science" amounts to virtue enlarged into piety: it reveals itself not only in social interest and human sympathy, honor, and justice, but also in gratitude, acquiescence,

---

which no theory can ever teach them." Similarly, "what is wrought in these men by the real disasters of life, may be supposed wrought in others by the fictions of tragedy; yet with this happy circumstance in favour of tragedy, that, without the disasters being real, it can obtain the same end.

"It must however, for all this, be confessed, that an effect of this kind cannot be reasonably expected, except among nations, like the Athenians of old, who lived in a perpetual attendance upon these theatrical representations. For it is not a simple or occasional application to these passions, but a constant and uninterrupted, by which alone they may be lessened or removed." Cf., however, *Phil. Inq.* II. vii, pp. 153–60, where the doctrine is quite different and comes somewhat closer to Aristotle's own.

42 Cf. *Phil. Inq.* II. xi, pp. 214–15.

43 *Thr. Tr. III.* ii. 9, p. 228.

resignation, adoration, and all that is owed by a man to the great universal polity "and its greater Governor, our common parent." [44] When "we are once . . . well habituated to this chief, this moral science, then logic and physics [especially] become two profitable adjuncts: logic, to secure to us the possession of our opinions; that if an adversary attack, we may not basely give them up: physics, to explain the reason and œconomy of natural events, that we may know something of that universe, where our dwelling has been appointed us." While this master-science is lacking, even logic must be valued "but as sophistry, and physics but as raree-shew; for both . . . will be found nothing better." [45] It is the supreme value of good poetry that it provides a means of developing this master-science through its accurate, just, and decent presentation of human life.

It is not difficult to see the similarity here to Harris' conception of the proper development of man's faculty of "remembering" the eternal ideas; his specific accounts of poetry and poems all reflect the controlling principle that there is a "congeniality" among good poetry, the true structure of reality, and the mind of man.[46] The point is not simply that

---

[44] *Ibid.* ii. 10, p. 248.

[45] *Ibid.*, p. 247. Cf. *Herm.*, Preface, pp. x–xi; III. iv. 3, pp. 392–97.

[46] The "principal delight" of imitations, as imitations, "is in recognizing the thing imitated" (*Thr. Tr. II.* iv. 3, pp. 80–81); and this is clearly proved by the fact that "we can be highly charmed with imitations, at whose originals in nature we are shocked and terrified." The reason for this is that we have "a joy, not only in the sanity and perfection, but also in the just and natural energies of our several limbs and faculties. And hence, among others, the joy in reasoning; as being the energy of that principal faculty, our intellect or understanding. This joy extends, not only to the wise, but to the multitude. For all men have an aversion to ignorance and error, and in some degree, however moderate, are glad to learn and to inform themselves.

"Hence therefore the delight, arising from these imitations; as we are enabled, in each of them, to exercise the reasoning faculty; and, by comparing the copy with the archetype in our minds, to infer that this is such a thing; and, that, another; a fact remarkable among children, even in their first and earliest days" (*ibid.*, pp. 80–81n.).

a poet **may** have and communicate philosophical knowledge or true moral precepts—although Ovid and Chaucer, and others, should be praised on that basis [47]—but that his work may *represent* the real character and order of things. Life itself is "one great important drama" [48] checkered with good and bad, true and false; and poetry, which imitates life, is of great and practical value when it properly mirrors the universal patterns of human ideas, actions, and passions. Even the "tragic" pattern, in which the sequence of events is from "good" to "bad," can, through our frequent contemplation, so habituate us to certain distressing and useless emotions that we become properly callous to them; it can do this because of our initial natural predisposition and ability to recognize ourselves in the characters and events depicted and to feel the emotions which ought to be "eradicated." [49] It is the true purpose of poetry, moreover, to be devoted in this way to the betterment of man. The "cause of letters [poetry and criticism], and that of virtue appear to co-incide, it being the business of both to examine our ideas, and to amend them by the standard of nature and of truth." [50] On this basis, Harris is able to argue, for example, that the English drama, "rationally cultivated" and properly improved, "might be made the School of Virtue even in a dissipated age." [51]

It is not completely clear, however, according to Harris' principles, whether the devices of poetry can ever be used with perfect success for manifestly erroneous and harmful purposes—consciously or unconsciously. For example, although misanthropy and atheism, he declares, are clearly erroneous and harmful, and when, as in the fourth book of *Gulliver's*

---

[47] See *Phil. Inq.* III. xi, pp. 468–72; *Phil. Arr.* VI, pp. 100–101.

[48] *Thr. Tr. III.* ii. 6, p. 210. See also *Phil. Arr.* X, pp. 244–51.

[49] See above, note 41. Cf. *Phil. Inq.* I. i, pp. 5–13; I. iii, p. 19; II. i, pp. 48–62.

[50] *Herm.* III. v, pp. 406–7.

[51] *Phil. Inq.* II. xi, p. 215.

Travels, they are overtly advanced there is real danger from the melancholy and morose character that may be formed by them—"morals and piety sink of course; for what equals have we to love, or what superior have we to revere, when we have no other objects left, than those of hatred, or of terror?" [52]— even Swift is unable to avoid the use of true human characteristics in his inhuman endeavor. Even, that is, in works overtly devoted to what Harris knows to be erroneous and harmful ends, the providential circulation of true reality can be discerned, and it renders quite ridiculous the poet who tries to oppose it. The last part of *Gulliver* is highly dangerous, "sapping the very foundations of morality and religion." [53] But, somewhat as Epicurus was a virtuous man in spite of his atheistic doctrines,[54] Swift was compelled to participate in the true scheme of things: "in order to render the nature of man odious, and the nature of beasts amiable, he is compelled to give human characters to his beasts, and beastly characters to his men—so that we are to admire the beasts, not for being beasts, but amiable men; and to detest the men, not for being men, but detestable beasts." [55]

But works of this sort are not thus vindicated. Although they might be loosely called "good" on the grounds of "wit" and technical "beauties" [56] (thus Harris concludes that Swift was a "wretched philosopher" but a "great wit"),[57] the crucial difference between a performance like Swift's and a really good poem (in the stricter sense of "good"), whether comic, tragic, or epic, is that the former directly imitates a false idea of human life, the latter a true one. Since its medium is

---

52 *Ibid.* III. xv, p. 537.
53 *Ibid.,* pp. 537–38n. He adds: ". . . I esteem the last part of Swift's *Gulliver* (that I mean relative to his *Hoyhnms* [sic] and *Yahoos*) to be a worse book to peruse, than those which we forbid, as the most flagitious and obscene."
54 *Ibid.* iii, p. 262.
55 *Ibid.* xv, p. 538n.
56 See *ibid.* II. x, pp. 184–205; III. xi, pp. 457–79.
57 *Ibid.* xv, p. 538n.

language, poetry can best imitate human action, character, thought, and feeling; and it is the proper, true imitation of these subjects which gives it its moral and metaphysical dignity and value. The terminology comes from Aristotle, but it is on the basis of ultimate moral truth, not merely of relative effectiveness in producing certain emotions, that Harris explains why it is a rule of tragedy, for example, not to present pre-eminently virtuous men as unfortunate, or notoriously infamous or unworthy beings as either fortunate or unfortunate: our natural sense of justice is offended by the one, our ability to recognize ourselves in a significant moral context is obviated by the other. Hence, in one of the most striking juxtapositions in the history of criticism, Harris argues that tragedy is at its supreme best as practiced by Sophocles (*Oedipus Rex*) and George Lillo (*The Fatal Curiosity*); there the true tragic form is clearly apprehended and consummately wrought.[58] A writer like Swift, in contrast, attempts, in his misanthropy and depravity, to violate the very basis upon which the value of poetry is determined—the proper depiction of real human life—and in so doing he vilifies not only the nature and rules of poetry but divine providence itself.

GENIUS AND THE MIND OF GOD

Harris views the universality and truth of the principles and rules of poetry as governed by the universality of human ideas, moral qualities, and languages and the unchanging character of the ultimate system of reality to which these human things naturally correspond. Upon this ground he bases his resolution of the familiar neoclassical opposition between "genius" and "rules."

It must be confest, 'tis a flattering doctrine, to tell a young beginner, that he has nothing more to do, than to trust his

---

[58] See *ibid.* II. vii, pp. 147–71.

own genius, and to contemn all rules, as the tyranny of pedants. The painful toils of accuracy by this expedient are eluded, for geniuses (like Milton's harps) are supposed to be ever tuned.

But the misfortune is, that genius is something rare, nor can he, who possesses it, even then, by neglecting rules, produce what is accurate. Those on the contrary, who, tho' they want genius, think rules worthy their attention, if they cannot become good authors, may still make tolerable critics; may be able to shew the difference between the creeping and the simple; the pert and the pleasing; the turgid and the sublime; in short, to sharpen, like the whet-stone, that genius in others, which nature in her frugality has not given to themselves.[59]

And he affirms that he has never known genius in any art to have been "crampt" by rules; on the contrary, he has seen "great geniuses miserably err by transgressing them, and, like vigorous travellers, who lose their way, only wander the wider on account of their own strength." [60] Swift was a great wit; but consider the filth and foolishness of *Gulliver's Travels.*

Yet Harris concedes that "in literary compositions, and perhaps more so in poetry than elsewhere . . . many things have been done in the best and purest taste, long before rules were established, and systematized in form." But it is far too easy to draw a wrong inference from these instances. Men will ask,

"If these great writers were so excellent before rules were established, or at least were known to them, what had they to direct their genius, when rules (to them at least) did not exist?"

To this question 'tis hoped the answer will not be deemed too hardy, should we assert, that there never was a time, when rules did not exist; that they always made a part of

59 *Ibid.* xii, pp. 222–23.
60 *Ibid.,* pp. 223–24.

that immutable Truth, the natural object of every penetrating genius; and that, if at that early Greek period, systems of rules were not established, those great and sublime authors were a rule to themselves. They may be said indeed to have excelled, not by Art, but by Nature; yet by a nature, which gave birth to the perfection of Art.[61]

He then proceeds to illustrate the natural genius of Shakespeare by pointing to the excellence of his characters and their sentiments. He draws an especially important similarity between the modes of reasoning of Hamlet and Socrates (the latter as recorded by Xenophon, Aristotle, and Horace), asserting that if "Truth be always the same, no wonder geniuses should co-incide, and that too in philosophy as well as in criticism." He adds that the "objections" to the performances of authors "are to be tried by the same rules, as the same plummet alike shews, both what is out of the perpendicular, and in it; the same ruler alike proves, both what is crooked, and what is strait." Then he focuses directly on the distinction between "rules" and "systems," which effects the resolution he has been working up to:

> We cannot admit, that geniuses, tho' prior to systems, were prior also to rules, because rules from the beginning existed in their own minds, and were a part of that immutable Truth, which is eternal and every where. . . .
>
> And this surely should teach us to pay attention to rules, in as much as they and genius are so reciprocally connected, that 'tis genius, which discovers rules; and then rules, which govern genius.
>
> 'Tis by this amicable concurrence, and by this alone, that every work of art justly merits admiration, and is rendered as highly perfect, as by human power it can be made.[62]

---

61 *Ibid.,* pp. 224–25.
62 *Ibid.,* pp. 225–32.

Although at the opening of his argument he accepts the commonplace opposition between untutored talent (genius) and established learnable rules of art, by shifting the meanings of the key terms he can allow "systems" of rules to remain separated from and external to the rare original genius, but the rules themselves to be seen both as part of the innate substance of genius and as the eternal laws by which its impulses are governed. The government of genius is thus government according to itself, and since the rules are a part of the one truth circulating through the universe, the development and control of genius is equivalent to the development and control of man's innate faculty of "remembering" the eternal forms.

The most important feature of this resolution of the genius-rules opposition is its employment of terms which belong specifically to what Harris usually calls "first philosophy," terms relating to matters of ultimate philosophical truth. He does not present the rules of art as merely accidental human conventions; they are basic elements of the true, divine order of the universe which is, after all, what the poet must apprehend. From this conception it would be easy to move to a doctrine of a special divine or natural inspiration by which the original unlearned genius acquires the proper rules (since he is prior to systems). But Harris does not do so; he defines the concepts commonly employed in discussions of inspiration —genius, enthusiasm, daimon, divine voice, holy spirit—so as to eliminate the idea of a special kind of supernatural influence from a higher being. In the third of the *Three Treatises,* a dialogue "Concerning Happiness," he extends the meaning of genius beyond his view of the powers of poetic production and of human learning to a conception of "mind" in general, using the term *genius* in this context interchangeably with δαίμων.[63] This is not an accident; his theory of universal gram-

---

[63] See *Thr. Tr. III* (Notes), p. 321.

mar turns in part on the doctrine that etymology is a source of proper meaning; [64] and his support for his theory of happiness includes (1) the connection between genius or daimon and "mind," and (2) the etymology of εὐδαίμων—"good mind." He notes that according to Aristotle (*Topics* II. vi) "Xenocrates held that he was *eudaemon,* or happy, who had a virtuous mind; for that the mind was every one's *daemon* or genius." Then he observes that here "we see virtue made the principle of happiness . . . . There is an elegant allusion [in Aristotle] . . . to the etymology of the word Εὐδαίμων which signifies both happy and possessed of a good genius or daemon." [65] Several pages later, he repeats the point in a slightly different way. "Daemon or genius means every man's particular mind, and reasoning faculty. . . . It is from this interpretation of *genius,* that the word, which in Greek expresses happiness, is elegantly etymologized to mean a goodness of genius or mind." [66]

The main significance of the connection which Harris draws between *genius* and *daimon* lies, nevertheless, in his view of the relation between individual minds and the mind of God, and therefore in the illumination which this might supply for an understanding of his conception of the poetic genius who was in one sense prior to, and in another sense "possessed" of, the rules of poetry. Human reason, he says, is "but a particle or spark, like some Promethean fire, caught from heaven above," of *general* rational mind,[67] and true happiness exists in the actual "harmony" which a man *can establish* between his own particular mind or "genius"

---

[64] See *Herm.* III. v, p. 407n.: "How useful to ethic science, and indeed to knowledge in general, a grammatical disquisition into the etymology and meaning of words was esteemed by the chief and ablest philosophers, may be seen by consulting Plato in his *Cratylus;* Xenoph. *Mem.* IV. 5, 6. Arrian. *Epict.* I. 17. Marc. Anton. III. 11. V. 8. X. 8."

[65] *Thr. Tr. III* (Notes), p. 321. Cf. *ibid. I.* v, pp. 41–42; *III.* ii. 8, pp. 214–22.

[66] *Ibid.* (Notes), p. 335.

[67] *Ibid.* ii. 9, p. 229.

and the mind of God; happiness is a dutiful—and rational—submission to God's order of things. Harris gives a character named Theophilus the task of expressing, with considerable rapture, the precise nature and importance of this harmonious submission:

> In as much as futurity is hidden from our sight, we can have no other rule of choice, by which to govern our conduct, than what seems consonant to the welfare of our own particular natures. If it appear not contrary to duty and moral office, (and how should we judge, but from what appears?) Thou canst not but forgive us, if we prefer health to sickness; the safety of life and limb, to maiming or to death. But did we know that these incidents, or any other, were appointed us; were fated in that order of incontroulable events, by which Thou preservest and adornest the whole, it then becomes our duty, to meet them with magnanimity; to co-operate with chearfulness in what ever Thou ordainest; that so we may know no other will, than thine alone, and that the harmony of our particular minds with thy universal, may be steady and uninterrupted thro' the period of our existence.[68]

But achieving this high level of resignation and cheerful submission seems to require assistance, in some sense, from the Almighty, and it is in this context that Harris introduces the concept of "enthusiasm." Two kinds of enthusiasm can be distinguished, one which corresponds to God's benevolent nature and order, and one which does not.

> Yet [continues Theophilus], since to attain this height, this transcendent height, is but barely possible, if possible, to the most perfect humanity: regard what within us is congenial to Thee; raise us above ourselves, and warm us into enthusiasm. But let our enthusiasm be such, as befits the

---

[68] *Ibid.*, pp. 231–32.

citizens of thy polity; liberal, gentle, rational, and humane
—not such as to debase us into poor and wretched slaves, as
if Thou wert our tyrant, not our kind and common father;
much less such as to transform us into savage beasts of prey,
sullen, gloomy, dark, and fierce; prone to persecute, to
ravage, and destroy, as if the lust of massacre could be grateful to thy goodness.[69]

Yet the better kind of enthusiasm is not presented explicitly
as "divine inspiration," and the works of Plato that might
have been brought in to support an idea of divine "possession," or special communication from the deity, do not appear. The notes to this passage refer us primarily to Epictetus,
Cleanthes, Chrysippus, Seneca, and the Stoics in general.[70]
Although Theophilus calls upon God for aid, he views the
proper enthusiasm as essentially rational and "humane"; it is
characterized not by irrational "possession" but by reasoned
devotion and consciously pursued virtue. The improper kind
of enthusiasm—"mad" and "savage"—simply lacks the essential qualities of calm resignation, submission, and devotion.[71]

There should be nothing surprising about this conception,
however. On the one hand, the etymology of the word *enthusiasm* does not absolutely require the notion of either irrational possession or special communication, and, on the other,
all truly rational minds, for Harris, are in direct communication with the mind of God when they possess ideas. There is
a sense, then, in which all rational philosophizing or intellectual activity may be said to be divine inspiration; God communicates his will to men in much the same way as men
communicate with each other—through an original "congeniality" of ideas. For "all minds, that are, are similar and congenial; and so too are their ideas, or intelligible forms."[72]

---

69 *Ibid.*, pp. 232–33.
70 *Ibid.* (Notes), pp. 336–37, 346–47.
71 Cf. *Ibid.* ii. 6, p. 211; *Phil. Inq.* III. xv, pp. 541–42.
72 *Herm.* III. iv. 3, pp. 395–400.

When in the proper state of enthusiasm, a man may be said to have a "good genius"—to be, that is, happy. If the aims of such a good genius are successful, it is thankful to providence; [73] but mere human success is not the source of true happiness, nor is true happiness a matter (in Pope's words) of "nameless graces" or of an uncertain and inexplicable "happiness as well as care" that must be dissociated from rational consciousness. Theophilus admits that the good genius "accepts all the joys" of mundane success and feels them as fully as anyone else.

> The only difference is, that having a more excellent good in view, it fixes not, like the many, its happiness on success alone, well knowing that in such case, if endeavours fail, there can be nothing left behind but murmurings and misery. On the contrary, when this happens, it is then it retires into itself, and reflecting on what is fair, what is laudable and honest (the truly beatific vision, not of mad enthusiasts, but of the calm, the temperate, the wise and the good) it becomes superiour to all events; it acquiesces in the consciousness of its own rectitude; and, like that mansion founded, not on the sands, but on the rock, it defies all the terrors of tempest and inundation.[74]

True happiness is the rational pursuit of a "steady, durable good" which (to be steady) must be derived from a "cause internal"; for the sovereign good of man must be placed in "mind," in "rectitude of conduct," in "just selecting and rejecting." [75] Hence Theophilus, after praying for the warmth of the proper kind of enthusiasm, speaks not of God's power to inspire or "fire" or "possess" him, but of his own task of "contemplation" of the intellectual forms of the providential circulation:

---

73 *Thr. Tr. III.* ii. 6, p. 211.
74 *Ibid.*
75 *Ibid.* ii. 7, pp. 212–13.

Here let us dwell;—be here our study and delight. So shall
we be enabled, in the silent mirrour of contemplation, to
behold those forms, which are hidden to human eyes—that
animating Wisdom, which pervades and rules the whole—
that Law irresistible, immutable, supreme, which leads the
willing, and compels the averse, to co-operate in their station to the general welfare—that Magic Divine, which by an
efficacy past comprehension, can transform every appearance, the most hideous, into Beauty, and exhibit all things
fair and good to Thee, Essence Increate, who art of purer
eyes, than ever to behold iniquity.[76]

Through all of this discussion of happiness and enthusiasm,
however, there is no special reference to poets. Harris' object
of concern here is man in general in his spiritual or mental
relation to the mind of God. Poetic genius, of course, may be
distinguished from human mind in general by the special
activity of writing poems; and thus it is possible to say, by
logical inference, that in Harris' scheme the truly happy poet
is one who performs in cheerful rational submission to the
divine order of things. "Genius" also signifies capacity to perform properly without consciousness of the system of divine
rules. But none of this implies a special kind of relation between the mind of the poet and the mind of God. The "original genius" in poetry, then, is apparently nothing more
astounding than a man with an exceptionally powerful and
sensitive mind who happens to write poems, a man unusually
well endowed with those innate mental powers possessed in
some degree by all men. It is proper to derive systems of rules
from the productions of the man of superior genius because
he is in this sense in harmony with the mind of God more
completely than most men.

One of the marks of a superior genius is the power of making good metaphors. It is a power that cannot be taught to

---

[76] *Ibid.* ii. 9, pp. 233–34.

someone lacking the necessary endowment, but it is grounded
on the common human process of perceiving analogies:

> There is not perhaps any figure of speech so pleasing, as the
> metaphor. 'Tis at times the language of every individual,
> but above all is peculiar to the man of genius. His sagacity
> discerns not only common analogies, but those others more
> remote, which escape the vulgar, and which, tho' they sel-
> dom invent, they seldom fail to recognise, when they hear
> them from persons, more ingenious than themselves.[77]

The greater poets, however, have proved their superior saga-
city not merely by their wit and their metaphors but in the
more important elements of their subject matter. Homer
had great command over metaphor,[78] but he was philosophical enough, whether through nature or art, to be quoted and
cited extensively (along with other great poets) in support of
the ten universal genera, and especially in regard to the doctrine of man's need for harmony with the will of God and the
doctrine of the providential circulation itself.[79] Shakespeare
too was a man of wisdom as well as a good poet in the sense
of being an accomplished maker of metaphors and other
beauties of "style." In the process of defining and illustrating
the very important genus of *relation,* Harris argues that the
knowledge of relations of various sorts is supremely important
in our task of achieving an upright and virtuous life and that
it is therefore essential to the "subordinate" task of the poet;
thus it is that Shakespeare performs his task of truly delineat-
ing human character and life:

> There are . . . [says the Stoic emperor Antoninus, following
> Epictetus and Ulysses] three relations; one to the proximate

---

[77] *Phil. Inq.* II. x, pp. 186–87.

[78] *Ibid.,* pp. 191–92n.

[79] See *ibid.* III. vii, pp. 351–53; *Phil. Arr.* I, p. 20; IV, pp. 80–81; VIII, pp.
145–46, 174; IX, pp. 210–11; X, pp. 221–22, 227–28n., 245–47; XII, p. 305;
XIII, pp. 335–37; XV, p. 375.

cause, which immediately surrounds us; one to the divine
cause, from which all things happen to all; and one to those,
along with whom we live. So important is the knowledge of
relations (according to these philosophers) in a subject,
which so much concerns us, I mean an upright and a virtuous conduct.

'Tis to a subordinate end, that Horace applies this knowledge, when he makes it an essential to dramatic poets, and
as a philosophical critic, teaches them, that 'tis thro' this
knowledge only they can truly delineate characters. . . .

'Tis thus too that Shakespeare, either by knowledge acquired, or (what is more probable) by the dictates of an
innate superior genius, makes Macbeth shudder at the
thoughts of murdering Duncan, when he reflects on the
many duties he owed him, arising from the many relations
he stood in, all of which duties he was then basely going to
violate. . . .

And here I cannot help remarking upon this excellent
tragedy, that it is not only admirable as a poem, but is perhaps at the same time one of the most moral pieces existing.
It teaches us the danger of venturing, tho' but for once,
upon a capital offence, by shewing us that 'tis impossible to
be wicked by halves; that we cannot stop; that we are in a
manner compelled to proceed; and yet that, be the success as
it may, we are sure in the event to become wretched and un-
happy.[80]

The argument does not extend explicitly beyond this, and we
are left to speculate whether Harris would encourage the great
genius to warm himself into "enthusiasm"—into a heightened
rational consciousness of his harmony with God's universe—
that he might better produce poems both "poetically" and
morally good. Certainly, it could do little harm.

---

[80] *Phil. Arr.* X, pp. 226–29.

ART AS POWER: HUMAN AND DIVINE

The difference between the superior genius and the common man—whether it is viewed in terms of the art of poetry or in terms of acquiring true happiness—involves not only a power of perceiving (or "recollecting") the true forms of reality but that of actively producing manifestations of those forms. The rules may be said to exist from the beginning, and to pre-exist in the mind of the original genius, but the poems must be written, the rules given concrete force in actual comedies and tragedies. The task of the first of Harris' *Three Treatises*, a dialogue "Concerning Art," is to discuss "art" in general, since it is "hardly probable . . . that music, painting, medicine, poetry, agriculture, and so many more, should be all called by one common name, if there was not something in each, which was common to all." [81] The central idea comes early in the dialogue; "art" is "an habitual power in man of becoming the cause of some effect, according to a system of various and well-approved precepts." [82] Into this conception Harris works his version of Aristotle's four causes. The efficient cause he has already presented, as the definition of art in general. The material cause or "subject" of art—the "common or universal subject"—is determined to be "all those contingent natures, which lie within the reach of human powers to influence." [83] The final cause—or "beginning" —of art, the cause "for the sake of which its several operations are exerted," is "the want or absence of something appearing good; relative to human life, and attainable by man, but superior to his natural and uninstructed faculties." [84] The formal cause—or "end"—of art is defined in terms of accomplishment, and this may be of two varieties, works or

---

81 *Thr. Tr. I.* i, p. 5.
82 *Ibid.*, p. 17.
83 *Ibid.*, p. 22.
84 *Ibid.* iii, p. 29.

energies: [85] "every art, according to its genius [i.e., special character], must needs be accomplished in one of these," and "except in these two, it can be accomplished in nothing else; and consequently . . . one of these must of necessity be its end." [86] But this staid, prosaic scheme is followed by a rapturous hymn to art in which its "dominion" is presented as extremely "wide and extensive," reaching to elements animate and inanimate, mental and material, and in which it is finally characterized as "mind" itself in its highest form. The hymn concludes:

> Hail! sacred source of all these wonders! Thyself instruct me to praise Thee worthily, thro' whom whate'er we do, is done with elegance and beauty; without whom, what we do, is ever graceless and deformed.—Venerable Power! By what name shall I address Thee? Shall I call thee ornament of mind; or art Thou more truly mind itself?—It is mind Thou art, most perfect mind; not rude, untaught, but fair and polished; in such Thou dwellest, of such Thou art the form; nor is it a thing more possible to separate Thee from such, than it would be to separate Thee from thy own existence.[87]

Art (efficient power), then, is the "form" of mind itself—that is, of "most perfect" mind. In *Philosophical Arrangements* Harris presents a similar dialectical view of efficient and formal causes in which "form" in the higher sense merges with the efficient power of art. He begins his explanation of the true being of animate natural substances (as part of his exploration of the universal genus *substance*) by drawing a somewhat fanciful picture of two artificial substances, musical

---

[85] Cf. Aristotle *Nicomachean Ethics* i. 1. 1094a1–5. Harris' account is somewhat confusing because of his use of the word *energies* here (which suggests efficient power) rather than, say, *activities*.
[86] *Thr. Tr. I.* iv, p. 36.
[87] *Ibid.* v, p. 42.

pipes and harps, and the special efficient powers necessary to
the "life" or "animation" of each:

> Let us suppose an artificial substance, for example a mu-
> sical pipe, and let us suppose to this pipe the art of the piper
> [i.e., the efficient cause] to be united, not separated as now,
> but vitally united, so that the pipe by its own election might
> play, whenever it pleased.—Would not this union render it
> a kind of living being, where the art would be an active
> principle, the pipe a passive, both reciprocally fitted for the
> purposes of each other?—And what, if instead of the piper's
> art, we were to substitute that of the harper?—Would this
> new union also be natural like the former? Or would not
> rather the inaptitude of the constituents prevent any union
> at all? It certainly would prevent it, and all melody conse-
> quent; so that we could now by no analogy consider the pipe
> as animated.
>
> 'Tis in these and other arts, considered as efficient habits,
> we gain a glimpse of those forms, which characterize not by
> visible qualities, but by their respective powers, their oper-
> ations and their energies. As is the piper's art to the pipe, the
> harper's to the harp, so is the soul of the lion to the body
> leonine, the soul of man to the body human; because in
> neither case 'tis possible to commute or make an exchange,
> without subverting the very end and constitution [formal
> cause] of the animal.
>
> And thus we are arrived at a new order of forms, the tribe
> of animating principles; for there is nothing which distin-
> guishes so eminently as these; and 'tis on the power of dis-
> tinction, that we rest the very essence of Form.[88]

In other words, we can "view form in a higher and nobler
light, than in that of a passive elementary constituent, a mere
inactive and insensible attribute"; we can view it, that is, in
the light of "the dignity of a living motive power destined by

---

[88] *Phil. Arr.* VI, pp. 95–98.

its nature to use, and not be used." [89] Form in this higher sense is not a sensible "element," not, for example, the Democritean tangible shape or "figure":

> As nothing can become known by that, which it has not, so it would be absurd to attempt describing these animating forms by any visible or other qualities, the proper objects of our sensations. The sculptor's art is not figure, but 'tis that, through which figure is imparted to something else. The harper's art is not sound, but 'tis that, through which sounds are called forth from something else. They are of themselves no objects either of the ear or of the eye; but their nature or character is understood in this, that were they never to exert their proper energies on their proper subjects, the marble would remain for ever shapeless, the harp would remain for ever silent. [90]

In the note to this passage, Harris cites Maximus Tyrius, "who eloquently applies this reasoning to the Supreme Being, the divine artist of the universe," and Shaftesbury, who has "elegantly translated" the original in his *Characteristics*. [91] The importance of this reference is obvious; what is true of the products of the human arts of (say) sculpture and harping is also true of "natural substances," which are the products of divine art: "The animating form of a natural body is neither its organization, nor its figure, nor any other of those inferior forms, which make up the system of its visible qualities; but 'tis the power, which, not being that organization, nor that figure, nor those qualities, is yet able to produce, to preserve, and to employ them." It is this power through which acorns become oaks, and the sick body cooperates with the medicine in effecting its cure: " 'Tis the power, which departing, the

---

[89] *Ibid.*, p. 98.

[90] *Ibid.*, p. 102.

[91] *Ibid.*, pp. 102–3n. Maximus Tyrius was a peripatetic philosopher in the the second century A.D.

body ceases to live, and the members soon pass into putrefaction and decay." And, what is more, "as putrefaction and decay will necessarily come, and nature would be at an end, were she not maintained by a supply; it is therefore the power, that enables every being to produce another like itself, the lion to produce a lion, the oak to produce an oak; so that, while individuals perish, the species still remains, and the corruptible, as far as may be, partakes of the eternal and divine." [92] We are then offered as the original artist of natural animate substances a quasi-Aristotelian "first mover" in radical contrast to a quasi-Aristotelian "prime matter," the "first" and the "last" objects of contemplation "in the general order of being." [93] In between is a scale of animate composites, on which man has high and independent station; beyond the instincts shared with other animals, "with man alone above the rest it is that still superior and more noble faculty, which by its own divine vigour, unassisted perhaps with organs, makes and denominates him a being intellective and rational." [94] Nevertheless, all the animating forms created by God "in their very essence . . . imply activity, as much as matter, upon which they operate, implies passivity." And it is in this way, as we learn from Virgil, "that to every enlivened substance, every animated being, there [is] something appertaining of etherial vigour, and heavenly origin, as far forth as not retarded by its mortal and earthly members." [95]

But here Harris tends to back away, perhaps from multiplying difficulties, and returns to a more general conception that can be supported without speculation about the exact details of the scale of being; it is sufficient for Harris' purposes

to mark the analogy between things natural and artificial; how, that as there are no Forms of art, which did not pre-

---

[92] *Ibid.*, pp. 103–5.
[93] *Ibid.*, p. 110.
[94] *Ibid.*, p. 106.
[95] *Ibid.*, pp. 109–10. The reference is to the *Aeneid* VI. 730–32.

exist in the mind of man, so are there no Forms of nature,
which did not pre-exist in the mind of God. 'Tis through
this we comprehend, how Mind or Intellect is the Region of
Forms, in a far more noble and exalted sense, than by being
their passive receptacle through impressions from objects
without. It is their region, not by being the spot into which
they migrate as strangers, but in which they dwell as
αὐτοχθόνες, the original natives of the country. 'Tis in mind
they first exist, before matter can receive them; 'tis from
mind, when they adorn matter, that they primarily proceed:
so that, whether we contemplate the works of art, or the
more excellent works of nature, all that we look at, as beautiful, or listen to, as harmonious, is the genuine Effluence or
Emanation of Mind.[96]

The "forms of art" which are highest and most important
are the efficient forms in the mind of the artist. Thus the
"analogy between things natural and artificial" turns mainly
in this context on an analogy between divine and human
forming power.

In the discussion of the categories or genera of *action* and
passion the doctrine that human art "imitates" divine art is
made explicit. Five "kinds" of action are distinguished and
arranged into a hierarchy. The first is that of mere body, as
in the burning of a substance, or the actions of chemicals.
The second is the action which results from sensation, instinct, and natural appetite, as in animals. The third is that
which results from reason, "superadded" to sensation, instinct, and appetite, and which thus may be called "moral"
action in the sense that the lower irrational faculties are intended to be subordinate to the superior faculty of reason.

There is a fourth sort of action, where the intellect, operating without passions or affections, stays not within itself,
but passes out (as it were) to some external operation. 'Tis

---

96 *Ibid.*, pp. 111–14.

thus that Nature, considered as an efficient cause, may be called the energy of God, seen in the various productions that replenish and adorn the world. 'Tis thus that Art, considered as an efficient cause, may be called the energy of man, which imitates in its operations the plastic power of Nature.

The last and most excellent sort of action is seen in contemplation; in the pure energy of simple intellect, keeping within itself, and making itself its own object. This is the highest action of which we are susceptible; and by it we imitate the Supreme Being, as far as is consistent with our subordinate nature. 'Tis to this that our great poet alludes, when speaking of his employment, during a state of blindness, he says—

> Then feed on thoughts, which voluntary move
> Harmonious numbers—— [97]

The divine action of contemplation, however, is not presented as a mode of "artistry," and human art or making, as such, imitates the divine efficiency or "plastic" power.

"Imitation" means difference, of course, as well as similarity. Although the great variety of sources upon which Harris draws for his descriptions of the divine artist makes it difficult to determine his special preference for one set of specific details, he apparently preferred a conception of God as possessing in his mind all the perfect immaterial forms of reality, both animate and inanimate, active and passive,[98] but operating as prime cause and eternal creator through pure activity,[99] which is opposed to pure passivity. Combined with this is a conception of divine creation *ex nihilo* and *in time* [100] (which perhaps explains the existence of the prime

---

[97] *Ibid.* XI, pp. 263–65.
[98] *Ibid.* XIII, p. 345.
[99] *Ibid.* XI, p. 271.
[100] See *ibid.* III, pp. 43–44. Cf. *Herm.* ("Additional Notes"), pp. 434–40 (citing Orpheus, Plato, Nicomachus of Gerasa, Proclus, Aquinas, and Milton). Harris does not view the creation in the Platonic terms of "imitation" and "persuasion," but he cites John Philoponus as treating the

matter or pure passivity upon which the divine being eternally operates) and the personalized attributes of omniscience, omnipotence, omnipresence, and omnibenevolence [101] (which are the enabling conditions of his "providential circulation"). As eternal creator and prime mover God is the "region" of all animate forms, but it is his will and power to maintain the providential circulation, especially in the active or animate forms of being. In contrast, the human artist, though essentially active and possessed of the a priori forms corresponding to the rules of his art, lacks the divine ability to give an animating form *as such* to any of his "subjects"; his instruments, his subjects, and his finished products, unlike those animated substances of the divine artist, cannot *exist* as permanent and self-reproductive unions of efficient, "formal," and material causes. The efficient principle of human art is always external to its materials and its final product.

Nevertheless, Harris arranges human arts into a hierarchy in terms of his identification of "art" with the highest active and efficient "form" of mind, and those arts (such as poetry) which exert their efficient powers of mind *upon* "mind" are at the top of the hierarchy and are most "divine." In other words, a distinction must be made between mind in general (but rational) and the efficient power of mind (somewhat as a distinction can be made between the animate and the inanimate—but rational—forms of all being existing in God's own mind); or, stated another way, rational mind passive (as matter) can be worked upon by rational mind active (as animating form). And although there is no indication that Harris views this as equivalent to producing a true union of efficient and material "form" (or animating form and matter), he

---

observable world of nature as an imperfect creature, one which falls short of the perfection of the eternal ideas in the mind of God. Nor does he give "matter" an independent existence prior to the creation of the world; yet he designates it as the passive ground of all created bodies.

101 See *Phil. Arr.* VIII, pp. 161–62; XII, pp. 313–14; XVII, pp. 450–51.

designates such artistry as truly "divine." One cannot question the general importance and nobility of the "lower" arts of the blacksmith, the carpenter, the musician and the maker of musical instruments, the shipbuilder and its pilot, the gardener, or the husbandman, where art is employed directly "on natures inanimate, or at best irrational" (which are clearly "inferior" subjects).

> But whene'er Thou choosest a subject more noble, and settest to the cultivating of Mind itself, then it is Thou [O human art] becomest truly amiable and divine; the ever flowing source of those sublimer beauties, of which no subject but mind alone is capable. Then it is Thou art enabled to exhibit to mankind the admired tribe of poets and of orators; the sacred train of patriots and of heroes; the godlike list of philosophers and legislators; the forms of virtuous and equal polities, where private welfare is made the same with public; where crowds themselves prove disinterested and brave, and virtue is made a national and popular characteristic.[102]

Harris speaks with particular favor (and obvious echoes of Shaftesbury) of the "moral artist" who is concerned to conduct *himself* according to a standard of human moral perfection. This standard of perfection or "exemplar" may be called "the true and perfect man: that ornament of humanity; that Godlike being." It is, unfortunately, "a perfection to which no *individual* ever arrived." But it *is* the perfection of human nature; and it is a part of true reality—it is not a fiction.[103]

---

[102] *Thr. Tr. I.* v, pp. 39–42.

[103] See *ibid. III.* ii. 1, pp. 188–91; ii. 8, pp. 214–22. See esp. p. 220, where the idea of perfection is identified with those "forms perhaps too perfect, ever to exist conjoined to matter," which are "yet as true and real beings, as the grossest objects of sense." Harris presents the idea of human perfection as pre-existing in the human mind, and, beyond this, he speaks approvingly of those philosophers who, conceiving the deity in moral

Harris does not bother to work out an account of the relative excellence of the various kinds of artists concerned with "mental" subjects. It is nevertheless clear that the poet, in his proper work, does not imitate the mere particulars of human life but rises, as do the true philosopher and the "moral artist," to the forms which are "general and comprehensive," the specific forms or a priori genera, thus becoming a "mind truly wise." [104] As God maintains the flow of existence by means of specific, not individual, forms,[105] so the poet has the power to give his works the specific comprehensive forms which correspond to the divine exemplars pre-existing in his mind. And because the poet is one who works upon materials or subjects that are mental to begin with, the materials of rational contemplation, he can be said to emulate God in the most exalted sense. Human artistry in general, however, is esteemable mainly for its power, not for its materials or its products; that is, although the works and energies of philosophers, poets, and statesmen are naturally more divine by virtue of their mental subjects than those of carpenters or husbandmen, all human artists may be said to partake of the analogy of human to divine art in terms of their efficient powers over matter and passivity.

Yet it is normally through the products that we are made aware of human artistic power, and thus of man's universal

---

terms that may be relevant to a description of human conduct, "have gone so far, as not to rest satisfied with the most perfect idea of humanity, but to substitute for our exemplar, even the supreme being, God himself. Thus Plato, in his *Theaetetus*, makes the great object of our endeavours, to be . . . the becoming like to God, as far as in our power. He immediately explains, what this resemblance is. . . . It is the becoming just and holy, along with wisdom or prudence" (*ibid.* [Notes], p. 339). Harris then adds references to Ammonius, Aristotle, and the Book of Matthew (5:48), remarking that he hopes that what has been said in the note will be "sufficient apology for the transcendence of the character described in the dialogue" (*ibid.*, p. 340).

104 *Ibid. III.* ii. 9, p. 227.
105 *Phil. Arr.* VI, pp. 105–6.

resemblance to God. The extant examples and records of
human art are valuable to us not only for their immediate
effects upon our individual and social lives but also for their
reflection of and testimony to the near-divinity of human
active mind; and these reflections and testimonies may be
found even in the most obscure and unenlightened periods
of human history—even in the medieval period:

> 'Tis surprising too, if we consider the importance of these
> various arts [of the "Dark Ages"], and their extensive utility,
> that it should be either unknown, or at least doubtful, by
> whom they were invented.
>
> A lively fancy might almost imagine, that every art, as it
> was wanted, had suddenly started forth, addressing those
> that sought it, as Eneas did his companions—
>
> —*Coram, quem quæritis, adsum.*
>
> And yet, fancy apart, of this we may be assured, that, tho'
> the particular inventors may unfortunately be forgotten, the
> inventions themselves are clearly referable to man; to that
> subtle, and active principle, human wit, or ingenuity.
>
> Let me then submit the following query—
>
> If the human mind be as truly of divine origin, as every
> other part of the universe; and if every other part of the
> universe bear testimony to its author: do not the inventions
> above mentioned give us reason to assert, that God, in the
> operations of man, never leaves himself without a wit-
> ness? [106]

Harris' profusely eclectic system of arguments thus works
its way back to the basic rationale for studying the products
of human art, especially the poetic and philosophical writings,
of all nations and ages. Harris is himself concerned to apprehend, organize, and present to the world the comprehensive
and universal forms of human art, the manifestations of the

---

[106] *Phil. Inq.* III. xiv, pp. 521–22.

highest powers of mind. His is a "dialectic of books," then, in the noble sense that it strives to demonstrate the providential circulation both of the one universal truth and of the active human mind's pervasive, unquenchable power to conquer recalcitrant matter and thus reveal its apprehension of ultimate reality and its harmony with the mind of God. To study the manifold writings of men is to study the broad, harmonious panorama of human art and genius, and this is also to study God's primary and universal witness of himself.

⊰ 6 ⊱

Varieties of Dialectical Theory

ALTHOUGH FULL-SCALE TRANSCENDENTAL OR comprehensive dialectic was not the predominant approach in England in the neoclassical period, fairly elaborate dialectical theories of poetry were developed, notably by Shaftesbury, Akenside, Hartley, and Harris, and together they represent a coherent and important aspect of English neoclassical criticism. There was a general tendency in this period to view all problems of knowledge, action, and aesthetics in relation to an examination of human mental faculties and processes; [1] and these four writers' conceptions of the general dialectical problem and their developments of the three Platonic themes may be viewed as different dialectical manifestations of this psychological emphasis. The differences, however, involve characteristics having no necessary or unique relation to this special tendency of the period, and they reveal a plurality of kinds of dialectic, not a simple unity of subject matter and method.[2]

In Shaftesbury's philosophy the general dialectical problem

---

[1] This is the historical fact upon which a number of studies of the origins of Romantic and "modern" criticism and aesthetics are based. See, e.g., J. G. Robertson, *Studies in the Genesis of Romantic Theory in the Eighteenth Century* (Cambridge, 1923); and, for more recent examples, Ernest Tuveson, *The Imagination as a Means of Grace* (Berkeley and Los Angeles, 1960), and L. A. Elioseff, *The Cultural Milieu of Addison's Literary Criticism* (Austin, Texas, 1963).

[2] For an instructive examination of varieties of dialectical philosophy in general, see McKeon, "Dialectic and Political Thought and Action," *Ethics,* LXV (1954), 1–33, esp. pp. 16–20.

centers on an internal conflict between the two parts of the human mind, the rational and the irrational, corresponding to the two aspects of nature. The resolution of this conflict is effected by a method of inward colloquy leading to a true knowledge of the self, which is equivalent to bringing into supremacy the higher rational part of the mind that corresponds a priori to the true forms of reality. For Akenside the dialectical problem entails, on the one hand, a distinction between the common "external" objects of taste or imagination and the higher spiritual or "mental" objects and, on the other hand, an opposition between matter and mind. The resolution of the former proceeds by means of the central powers of the human imagination itself, which can range between the lower and the higher by virtue of the pervasiveness of the idea of beauty especially, whereas the resolution of the latter is effected by a supplementary process of "association," by which "mental" qualities can be attributed to "material" things. In Hartley's system the dialectical problem, reflected in the radical difference between the two parts of his work, involves an opposition between "nature" and "heaven" and thus between man's lower faculties and behavior as a fallen creature and his higher faculties and duty to conform to the will of God. The resolution of this opposition is effected partly by the doctrine of the "necessity" of intellectual "associations" and partly by the postulation of a special grace, a special given inclination in some men toward faith in Christ, that enables the mechanical process of association to lead them in the direction of conforming to God's will, providing thus a practical means by which the behavior of men in general may be properly regulated. For Harris the dialectical problem turns on an opposition between common unassisted experience of the world and the one universal truth which gives reality to the experienceable world and validity to human thought about it. The resolution is found in the doctrine of the "congeniality" of the human mind and its universal grammar and logic with the providential circulation or continuing emanation of active spiritual forms from the mind of God and thus in the scholarly process of perceiving and organizing the "reflections" of the providential circulation in the writings of men. Shaftesbury's is thus a dialectic of the rational self; Akenside's is a dialectic of imaginative perception or vision; Hartley's is a dialectic of necessary salvation by faith and obedience; and Harris' is a dialectic of divine philology. The four are united by the common quest for an identity or a parallelism between the true or ultimate order of things and the ideas, actions, and feelings of men.

THE TRUE NATURE AND VALUE OF POETRY

When the subject is the nature and value of poetry and the poet, the dialectic is specified in terms which relate the poet and his work to ultimate reality and to social usefulness in the context of ultimate reality. According to Shaftesbury poetry ideally not only can accurately depict the higher "active" forms of beauty but also can imitate the inward colloquy itself, which is the essential method of philosophy; hence "dramatic" poems, which resemble dialogues, are superior to other poetic forms, and the poet can best perform his task of "improvement"—of himself and others—in the dramatic manner. In Akenside's conception, the poetic power of imagination, occupying a middle position between bodily sense and the faculties of moral perception but extending its purview to both, unites the higher moral excellencies of life with the mere external objects of good taste chiefly by perceiving and rendering the pervasive "divine form" of Beauty, which at the highest level of "expressive" mind coalesces with virtue and truth. For Hartley the poet, though inferior in general to the scientist, may accurately imitate observable nature and thus avoid untoward interference with the "necessary" processes of association established for man by God; and, although the or-

dinary heathen and modern kinds of poetry are highly corrupting, the poet may also, God willing, so select and arrange his
subject matter as to promote the welfare of mankind and the
glory of God. Harris argues that the poet may achieve, and
help his readers to achieve, a kind of "moral science," which
is prior in importance to other sciences, by apprehending or
"remembering" the universal or true forms of human life and
representing them accurately and effectively. Thus all four
dialecticians conceive the poet as positively useful to man in
society. The differences among their special accounts of his
cognitive and moral power are found primarily in the differences among their conceptions of the true nature of things
and of the special kind of parallelism or conformity which can
be discovered or established between that reality and the
mind of man in general; for the poet is distinguished from
other men, if at all, by the greater or lesser degree in which
he may manifest or actualize a positive relation to reality, not
by any basic peculiarity of *kind* of mind or feeling.

The relation of the poet's mind to the mind of God or to
the spiritual principle of the higher reality is, nevertheless, a
common theme. Shaftesbury treats the question of divine inspiration somewhat skeptically; but nature may be said to
"enchant" and inspire, and "enthusiasm," or the "feeling" of
divine inspiration, may be related to a true rather than false
conception of the divinity and thus be of real practical value
to poets. The great poetic "genius," however, is not defined as
inspired by God, since man's greater artistic achievements are
accompanied not by passive and irrational possession but by
active, rational, self-knowledge. Akenside, on the other hand,
speaks of the inspiration which the poet may receive from the
divine form of Beauty herself as well as from the great poetic
works of antiquity, and the poet is impassioned, "fired," and
"frenzied" when he works, since Parnassus cannot be con-
quered by dull and "creeping" prose; the inspiration of
Beauty is "received" by the poet's faculty of imagination or

fancy, and poets are more richly endowed in this faculty than common men. Hartley argues that only the divine scriptures are inspired in the sense of being the word of God; but poets may hope, as men, to be given a special enabling grace, an inclination toward conformity to true religion, and they may hope at the same time to avoid "enthusiasm," the false belief that one is a special favorite of God. Faith, moreover, is essentially irrational, and reason is the characteristic natural faculty of man as fallen creature. Harris, in contrast, defines proper "enthusiasm" as a rational and deliberate heightening of one's harmony with the mind of God, and a doctrine of special "possession" or irrational inspiration is unnecessary, if not impossible, since all human minds are originally in essential harmony with the divine ideas; hence, the opposition between the natural poetic "genius" and the "rules" of poetry can be resolved by finding both to be in harmony with the providential circulation of the one universal truth.

When the divinity is conceived in terms of a being making, building, or "producing"—as in both the Hebraic-Christian and the Platonic-Stoic cosmologies—it is not difficult to view the human maker or poet as analogous to God himself. The analogy may take various forms, depending on the particular theorist's conception of the poet and of the nature of God's creativity. According to Shaftesbury, the human poet may be termed a "second maker" in the sense that his "dramatic" productions are analogous to the productions of God and of God's "substitute" Nature, and especially in the sense that through his poetry he may "give birth" to "better" minds. His productiveness differs, thus, from ordinary human reproduction in being directed to the making of *mental* forms in human beings that correspond to the divine spiritual forms according to which the concrete universe was initially created and is continued by Nature. Akenside conceives poetry—or "mimic art" in general—in terms of powers of "forming" or "organizing" in a sense which makes the analogy between human imagination and divine creative power seem inevitable, and each part of his description of mimic art is paralleled by an aspect of his description of the Sire Omnipotent's "expressive" creation and continuing maintenance of the universe; the true poet or "child of fancy" is capable of experiencing a rapturous harmony with the divine order of things, and it is when he is enjoying this experience that his forming power may result in products which rival in value even God's own created universe. In Hartley's scheme the analogy appears largely in a negative form. Common heathen and modern poets are noted chiefly for the destructive consequences of their works, though particular poets may be constructive (and thus somewhat God-like), if God allows, by "concurring" with His benevolent design. Man is incapable, however, of real creation, the kind of absolute creation out of nothing which may be attributed to God, and the poet's "invention" can be reduced to a mechanical accumulation of "associations." Harris views man as partly a passive creature, God as wholly active; yet man is capable of "art" or efficient power identical in kind with God's own active power, and thus the products of human art, especially those wrought in language, may be called God's primary witness of Himself.

For all four writers an analogy (positive or negative) between human and divine artistry or productiveness provides the final criterion for the determination of the social and philosophic value of poetry and the poet, because all four define the true reality of the universe by reference to the form, conception, will, or active idea of a creative God. And it is primarily in terms of the degree to which the poet may resemble, approximate, or "concur" with this God in the apprehension and materialization of the divine will or idea that his value in the true order of things must be established.

THE RANGE OF NEOCLASSICAL DIALECTIC

The four theories are typically "neoclassical" in the sense that they share the common psychological emphasis and much of the common critical language characteristic of a period conventionally given that name. In a somewhat less conventional sense, however, they provide a representative picture of the dialectical aspect of English neoclassical criticism because they were developed in large part out of a wide and representative range of the period's conceptual and doctrinal materials. Among these, topics and principles derived from classical rhetoric and rhetorically oriented poetic theory were taken seriously by all four writers; and all four particularly tended to view the production of poems in a classical rhetorical way—that is, as an artistic combination of subject matter to be communicated *(inventio)* and method or manner of doing it *(dispositio* and *elocutio)*. The conceptual materials, principles, and problems of the rhetorical tradition were of special positive importance, however, to Shaftesbury and Akenside in the actual construction of their dialectical schemes, although Shaftesbury occasionally drew upon other non-dialectical traditions, and Akenside strove hard to assimilate certain concepts current in the empirical tradition of Locke and Addison also. Hartley, on the other hand, especially made extensive positive use, in the actual construction of his "system," of principles and doctrines that came most directly from causal-empirical philosophies of the period. And Harris was unusually fond of the ideas as well as the works of "the philosopher" Aristotle.

Neither Shaftesbury's nor Akenside's theory of poetry, of course, is rhetorical in the sense of being limited to questions of propriety and effectiveness as determined by "merely human" social standards; although Shaftesbury's theory may be described succinctly as one which develops the "rational" or "judicial" side of the Horatian distinction between *ingenium* and *sapere,* and Akenside's as one which develops the imaginative, less rational side, both tasks are accomplished in transcendental terms. Similarly, Hartley's elaboration of the principle of mechanical association of ideas is singularly thorough, but finally it is given its essential significance by a priori religious concepts and doctrines in a distinctly un-empirical way; he embraces the "Democritean" principle of mechanism and habit as the means of defining human nature after the Fall and as the grounds for subordinating human rational choice to the power of God and to revelation and faith. Harris' use of Aristotle is as pious as Hartley's use of either Locke or the Bible, but he subordinates Aristotle's concepts and definitions, often in radically altered form, to those of a variety of Neoplatonists and Stoics, developing his philological dialectic in part by giving "ideal" exemplary status to Aristotle's substantial forms and categories of predication. Nevertheless, it is clear that basic differentiating constitutive materials for these dialectical theories are provided by the three kinds of non-dialectical theory.

These tendencies are reflected, moreover, in the discursive and literary procedures which the four writers employed. Shaftesbury's own works are often dialogues, "soliloquies," or miscellaneous reflections conceived chiefly as modes of persuasion which imitate, in a concrete social manner, his ideal of the rational inward colloquy, whereas Akenside was a "child of fancy" by avocation and discussed the nature and value of poetry in a long rhetorical poem designed to "enlarge," "harmonize," and effectively illustrate, as well as state, the powers of imagination. Both parts of Hartley's treatise are done in the "mathematical" manner of seventeenth-century philosophers, and they reflect with remarkable clarity, in style as well as substance, the main parts of his dialectic—the mechanical processes of nature and the will of God. Although Harris' works are always eclectic and "scholarly," filled with citations of authority and quotations in Greek and Latin which demonstrate the providential circulation of eternal ideas, he wrote in a number of conventional forms in his effort to solve dialectically a number of common critical problems raised by dialectical and non-dialectical theorists alike.

It is possible thus to discern in these four writers three basic varieties of dialectical theory, distinguished according to the kinds of *non*-dialectical principles and issues which each took most seriously in his dialectical act of confronting, adopting, and developing the various ideational materials and literary procedures available to him: Shaftesbury and Akenside a quasi-rhetorical "Horatian" variety (in two primary sub-forms or emphases), Hartley (and Akenside in a secondary way) a quasi-causal "Democritean" variety, and Harris a quasi-problematic "Aristotelian" variety. And it is in this sense that they may be said to mark out the full range of the dialectical aspect of English neoclassical criticism.

The central common problem for which the four theories provide solutions, or at least approximations of solutions, is that of how the poet may be properly related both to a higher reality and to the practical affairs of human life, without being required to succumb completely to the standards and forces of sublunary nature. The solutions are not identical because the precise definitions of the problem and the modes of solving it are not identical; but the four schemes share in a general sense the Stoical principle of the human need to adjust positively to the actual circumstances of life in a world that is less perfect than what human beings themselves can imagine and desire, and these theories of poetry are all attempts to give the poet a role in human social life in which he may contribute supremely, or at least significantly, to the guidance and culture, the salvation, or the happiness of men according to the true principles of the world of which they are organic parts. The problem of man's relation to the higher reality is defined, indeed, in generally psychological terms (as distinct from ontological ones), and the special value of poetry is defined chiefly in terms of the "heuristic" processes of imitation, imaginative vision, association and invention, and recognition and recollection by which the poet produces the subject matter of his poems, not in terms of the reality or unreality of the concrete things which poets make; but the broadly psychological and rhetorical focus does not prevent analogizing human poetic products of the better sort to the creations of God on the basis of those higher forms and substances (dramatic, expressive, revealed, and intellectual) which the poet is able to understand, receive by inspiration, or actively develop.

THE UNIVERSALITY OF DIALECTICAL THEORY: SOME RECENT PARALLELS

The result, in effect, is a group of neoclassical "defenses" of poetry, formulated on the basis of the classical Platonic issues which have been raised recurrently (and surely will continue to be raised) in the history of criticism. Dialectical methods were common among medieval discussions of poetry from Augustine to Petrarch and Boccaccio, and significant dialectical theory and criticism was produced in the Renaissance—by Julius Caesar Scaliger, Gosson and Sidney, Spenser, and by Milton, among others. Dialectical concerns and reasoning and an especial emphasis on the theme of resemblance between human poetic production and divine creativity are essential marks of most of the major poetic theories produced in the "Romantic" period—of those of Goethe, Schelling, Schiller, the Schlegels, and of Wordsworth and Coleridge.[3] In this broader perspective the four theories may be said to reveal not only the range of dialectical theory in the neoclassical pe-

---

[3] See Appendix, below, pp. 187–209. There is no general history of dialectical criticism, but McKeon's "Imitation and Poetry," in *Thought, Action, and Passion*, pp. 102–221, "Poetry and Philosophy in the Twelfth Century: The Renaissance of Rhetoric," in *Critics and Criticism*, pp. 297–318, and "The Philosophic Bases of Art and Criticism," in *ibid.*, pp. 463–545 contain useful materials.

riod but also some of the universal features of one of the major forms of theorizing about poetry which men may develop at any time.

Such universal features are not, however, a matter of critical vocabulary or of specific doctrines about poetry; they are characteristics of problem and method, discernible, if we are prepared to discern them, irrespective of any similarities or differences of vocabulary or doctrine that may exist among men and ages. It seems clear, for example, that most of the dialectical criticism in our own period is developed out of terminological and doctrinal materials generally different from those typical of the neoclassical period. It is perhaps illuminating, therefore, that all three varieties of dialectical poetics explored here may be perceived, without great imaginative effort, among noted dialectical critics of our time writing in English: the two forms or emphases ("rational" and "imaginative") of the quasi-rhetorical variety in Yvor Winters' conception of the poet as a constructor of statements about experience which must be judged in terms of a comprehensive system of rational-theological morality [4] and in I. A. Richards' attribution of a supra-scientific social function (for the "suitable reader") to the non-rational, "pseudo-statement" powers of imagination; [5] the quasi-causal variety in T. S. Eliot's combination of mechanistic affectivism and religious historicism; [6] and the quasi-problematic variety in Northrop Frye's eclectic treatment of a providential circulation of universal modes, symbols, archetypes, and genres which govern the nature and value of poetry. [7]

---

[4] See, e.g., *In Defense of Reason* (Denver, Colorado, 1947), pp. 21–22; *The Function of Criticism: Problems and Exercises* (Denver, 1957), pp. 160–61.

[5] See *Science and Poetry* (New York, 1926), *passim; Coleridge on Imagination* (London, 1934), pp. 219–33.

[6] See, e.g., "Hamlet and His Problems," "Tradition and the Individual Talent," and "Religion and Literature," in *Selected Essays* (New York, 1950), pp. 121–26, 3–11, 343–54.

[7] *Anatomy of Criticism, Four Essays* (Princeton, 1957), *passim.* Cf. *The Well-Tempered Critic* (Bloomington, Ind., 1963), esp. pp. 121–45, 153–56.

These cases are chosen in part for their special resemblances to Shaftesbury and Akenside, Hartley, and Harris; but of course the parallels are severely limited by the peculiarities of modern critical vocabulary and by individual principles and doctrines. For example, Winters does not adopt the dualistic "dramatic" and representational emphasis which was basic to Shaftesbury; Richards, unlike Akenside, fails to find a satisfactory way in which the poet in our time can be related to divine ideas as well as to the noble task of "harmonizing" our attitudes and impulses; [8] Eliot's institutional scheme of salvation is quite different from Hartley's; and Frye's universal forms involve conceptions of depth psychology and primitive ritual that Harris probably would not readily understand. In a more general sense, moreover, modern dialectical critics, unlike their neoclassical counterparts, tend to concentrate almost entirely on one of the three dialectical themes, the special power, need, or tendency of the poet to understand, apprehend, or represent the truth that is most relevant to human life—the theme, that is, of the poet as dialectician or lawgiver. And indeed we might expect the themes of divine communication and of the analogy between human and divine creativity to have somewhat lessened significance as the reality of "mind," divine or human, tends to be increasingly found in analysis of the natural causes of structures of verbal meaning, and "scientific" cosmology takes the place of creation myth. Nevertheless, the dialectical mode of thought persists, and some contemporary critics have seriously attempted to keep alive also the themes of poetic inspiration and resemblance to divine creativity—for example, W. K. Wimsatt, Jr.,

---

8 Like Akenside, Richards employs a number of "empirical" scientific concepts and terms, within a dialectical framework, as means of understanding and describing the poet's appropriate or proper subject matter but subordinates them to the better and the worse solutions of essentially rhetorical-social problems, the problems primarily of communication and psychological influence and control, in terms of which the poet's fundamental artistic task is discussed.

in his argument that poetry, as speaking picture (or "verbal icon") and as analogue of the Christ, is a "tensional union of making with seeing and saying"; [9] Wallace Stevens, in his conception of the power of reality to "reveal" itself to and "transport" the "humble" poetic spirit, who acts as a kind of intermediary between that reality and the audience; [10] and Jacques Maritain, in his neo-Thomistic theory of "creative intuition." [11]

---

[9] See *Literary Criticism: A Short History*, pp. 740–55.
[10] See, e.g., *The Necessary Angel* (New York, 1951), pp. 47–51, 99–103.
[11] *Creative Intuition in Art and Poetry* (New York, 1955); see esp. pp. 51–108.

Our period, especially in English-speaking countries, bears some general similarities to the England of the late seventeenth and eighteenth centuries; ours too is an age in which, to use the more recent terms, the activities of pragmatism, psychologism and positivism, and literal analysis are extremely vital forces. But the dialectical reaction against these nondialectical forms of activity seems to be stronger and more widespread today than it was in the "enlightenment" of the eighteenth century. Thus, on a more widespread basis, it tends to divide our intellectual universe into something like what C. P. Snow and F. R. Leavis have recently debated under the rubric "two cultures"; and when there are only two parts, such as "poetry" and "science," in man's universe the chances are good that the "poetry" side of the disjunction will frequently be treated (by the critics, the lovers, and the producers of poetry, if not so frequently by the men of action, the scientists, and the scholars) in a way that preserves the importance of both realms of human effort, but gives the final nod to poetry.

There is little reason, in any case, to fear that the dialectical approach to poetry, and the kinds of values to which it calls our attention, will be eliminated or even much hampered by the tendencies of pragmatism, positivism, and literal analysis evident in our time—any more than they were by like tendencies in the eighteenth century. There is indeed perhaps more reason to fear today that the concern on the part of both poets and critics with the task of relating poetry to a higher reality or truth or to the ultimate welfare of mankind (so that it may better compete with "science") will come more and more to obscure, by transformation, submersion, or corruption, those potential tasks, properties, and values of human literary art which an interest in the characteristic problems of nondialectical theories may enable us to recognize and take seriously. (Among the more prominent contemporary critics, R. S. Crane, Elder Olson, and their followers have done problematic criticism on a systematic basis; Kenneth Burke offers an elaborate and thoroughgoing instance of the rhetorical approach; and George Santayana and George Boas present fairly

It must be emphasized, however, that the perception of such
parallels is not an act of recognizing the natural or providential circulation of eternal metaphors or "unit ideas"; it is an
act of recognizing the recurrence, in the intellectual efforts of
individual men, of *formative* dimensions of human theory,
dimensions which reflect the human action of solving specific
theoretical problems—the action by which theories actually
come into being. One reason why the dialectical aspect of English neoclassical criticism, paralleling the dialectical modes
found in other periods, has not been much examined before
is surely the fact that the individual writers who carried on
the tradition have been found intrinsically less interesting and
less readable than some of the non-dialectical thinkers of the
period such as Dryden, Pope, Hume, and Johnson; but another is the general tendency among modern scholars to look
only at the material dimensions of theory—and, ironically, to
do so largely within dialectical historical frameworks of their
own. This essay has been developed on the hypothesis that
adequate understanding of the intellectual characteristics of
the theories of any period requires a genuinely problematic
method, a method in which the historian moves beyond questions of critical terminology and isolated statements about
poetry to a systematic analysis of individual theories in terms
of different kinds of problems and methods of solving them
—in terms of the forms of theory, in their several varieties,
which men have developed—and attempts to do so in a free
spirit of inquiry, eschewing the control of special assumptions
either about the one universal nature of all theorizing or
about the sorts of theorizing which must or must not be found

---

clear examples of the causal approach. All are remarkably capable of
performing independently of the problems and procedures of dialectical
poetics, and it is probably not an accident that they have been rather
isolated from the main "establishment" of modern American and British
criticism—Burke somewhat less so than the others, perhaps because it is
easier, in general, to confuse an elaborate rhetorical method with the
method of trancendental or comprehensive dialectic.)

in any particular age or "episode" in history. The analysis of these four dialectical theories of poetry produced in the neoclassical period provides a convenient illustration and perhaps a useful test of the method.

Appendix

DIALECTICAL PROBLEMS AND ROMANTIC THEORY: S. T. COLERIDGE

> ... with increasing emphasis and frequency, poetry
> becomes a part of divine creation, a smaller parallel
> to the work of art which is nature.
>
> RENÉ WELLEK, *The Romantic Age*

IT HAS OFTEN BEEN NOTED THAT ONE OF THE BROADER developments in English criticism toward the beginning of the nineteenth century involved a shift in dominant interest and theoretical starting point among the majority of critics away from the questions of achieving or explaining effects upon the audience to questions of the productive psychology of the author.[1] The focus on different "forms" of poetic theory provides a framework for discussing this development in terms of intellectual causes and motives rather than merely of accidental differences of critical subject matter and language. The rhetorical and causal theories which dominated neoclassical criticism were primarily audience-oriented, even when they concerned themselves (as they frequently did) with the mind and habits of the poet also. The dialectical theories, on the other hand, concentrated primarily on the relation of the

---

[1] See, e.g., R. S. Crane, "Neoclassical Criticism: An Outline Sketch," in *Critics and Criticism*, pp. 386–88; Abrams, *The Mirror and the Lamp*, p. 29. See also "Neoclassical Poetics," *Encyclopedia of Poetry and Poetics*, ed. Alex Preminger (Princeton, 1965), pp. 559–63.

poet's mind and productive processes to the ultimate reality which gives meaning and value to all things, even when they concerned themselves (as they commonly did) with questions also of audience psychology. Hence it may be possible to argue that the general shift of dominant interest in the nineteenth century away from the audience to the mind of the poet was part of a more fundamental shift from non-dialectical to dialectical theory. The technical and analytic issues characteristic of rhetorical, causal, and problematic theories may always be discussed without making the mind and productive activity of the poet the center of attention or starting point; but when the general task is to defend poetry against, or to attack it in terms of, the claims of practical action, science, or religious dogma and to do so by relating it dialectically to a higher reality or truth, there is strong likelihood (especially in a period when human activities in general are most often viewed in terms of psychological and epistemological data and problems) that the critic will find himself centrally concerned with questions of the cognitive, expressive, and creative powers and processes of the poet.

To explain why this shift to a predominant interest in the problems of dialectical theory should have occurred in the first place would require extensive exploration of social and intellectual tendencies and developments which go beyond the history of poetic theory as such. And it may be seriously doubted that such general historical explanations are possible at all in terms of actual human intellectual activity.[2] Obvious similarities, however, between the four neoclassical dialectical conceptions of poetic invention and those typical of the Ro-

---

[2] The best critical examinations of causal and dialectical theories of history of which I am aware are William Dray's *Laws and Explanation in History* (Oxford, 1957) and Karl Popper's *The Poverty of Historicism* (London, 1957). Cf. McKeon, *Freedom and History* (New York, 1952) and "Truth and the History of Ideas," in *Thought, Action, and Passion,* pp. 54–88.

mantic period tend to make the question of intellectual continuity unavoidable; and this is something that can be discussed in terms of human action and choice, if we concentrate on the work of an individual Romantic theorist. There are a number of especially suggestive "material" similarities between the four neoclassical theories and the dialectical theory of Samuel Taylor Coleridge: [3] Shaftesbury's concern with knowledge of the true self, with the idea of duality as a fundamental principle of being and philosophy, and with the idea of strife or struggle in the finite processes of the human mind, and his conception of true beauty as involving not merely "dead" structure but forming power; Akenside's decision to start from the "faculties" of the human mind and his insistence on the "divine" expressive and creative "harmonizing" powers of imagination; Hartley's dialectical distinction between the "liberal arts" and "science," his conception of the close parallel between the "languages" of imagination and morality, and his final submersion of all human activities in Christ; and Harris' emphasis on the principle of "congeniality" between the human and the divine and particularly on the God-like *active* power of human art. There are many other similarities of this sort; a full survey and analysis of them would require a large separate study, but their existence is patent, and they point to aspects of Coleridge's intellectual relations with his immediate English predecessors in poetic theory which have not been adequately examined.[4]

---

[3] As guides to my reading of Coleridge I have found the following two recent works especially valuable: R. H. Fogle, *The Idea of Coleridge's Criticism* (Berkeley and Los Angeles, 1962) and J. D. Boulger, *Coleridge as Religious Thinker* (New Haven, 1961).

[4] Coleridge's preoccupation with Hartley's system is of course well known. Whether he had read much of Shaftesbury, however, is not clear. In his letter to John Thelwall of 13 May 1796 (*Collected Letters of Samuel Taylor Coleridge*, ed. E. L. Griggs [Oxford, 1956], I, 214) he mentions "Lord Shaftesbury" and Rousseau as examples of non-Christians whose disciples can nevertheless be true patriots. This is probably the *Third Earl*, though Griggs does not indicate any difference between this reference

The special uses, however, which a dialectical critic of the Romantic period made of terms, ideas, and arguments available to him in the works of other men must be expected to follow the same processes of reaction, incorporation, and mod-

---

and the two clear references in other letters (II, 701 and IV, 758) to the First Earl, and the case is not obvious. There are numerous admiring references to Akenside and citations of his works, the full significance of which has not been explored. See *The Notebooks of Samuel Taylor Coleridge*, ed. K. Coburn (New York, 1957), 123, 123n.; *Collected Letters*, I, 215, 230, 279, 289, 307; III, 361. There are also favorable references to Harris, indicating at least that Coleridge was sympathetic toward the kind of work which Harris had done, and it is quite possible that he actually made theoretical use of specific ideas which he found in Harris' writings. See *Biographia Literaria*, ed. J. Shawcross (London, 1907), II, 26n.; "Table Talk" (May 7, 1830) in *Complete Works of Samuel Taylor Coleridge*, ed. W. G. T. Shedd (New York, 1853), VI, 308; the works which Coleridge alludes to at these places are *Philological Inquiries* and *Hermes* respectively. In the very interesting letter to Josiah Wedgwood, 18 February 1801 (*Collected Letters*, II, 679), he mentions Harris and Monboddo on the subject of Locke's ignorance and misunderstandings of ancient philosophy, particularly of the ancient doctrine of innate ideas. Coleridge's conclusion is not essentially different from Harris'—though it is arrived at and supported with a much more incisive and perceptive process of inquiry and argument than Harris reveals. It is perhaps an important fact that references to Harris and Monboddo occur at this very crucial point in Coleridge's intellectual life, when he is beginning successfully to "overthrow" the "doctrine of Association, as taught by Hartley, and with it all the irreligious metaphysics of modern Infidels—especially, the doctrine of Necessity" (Letter to Thomas Poole, 16 March 1801 [*Collected Letters*, II, 706]).

There is no suggestion here that we should doubt the significance of non-English thinkers, especially the German "Sturm-und-Drangers" and idealists of the eighteenth and early nineteenth centuries, or of other English philosophers, particularly the Cambridge Platonists, Berkeley, and physio-theologists like John Ray and Joseph Butler, in the development of English Romantic theory. But few of these Englishmen concerned themselves much with problems of the nature and value of poetry specifically, and a good deal still needs to be discovered about the importance of English writers in the development of the German "Aufklärung" and "Idealismus." The following works provide especially pertinent treatments of this latter subject (all, unfortunately, from a terminological, phraseological, or merely doctrinal point of view): G. J. ten Hoor, "Akenside's *The Pleasures of Imagination* in Germany," *Journal of English and Germanic Philology*,

ification discovered among the four neoclassical dialecticians; [5] and, indeed, writers are commonly moved to thoughts, actions, or creations by conceptual and doctrinal antecedents which they find abhorrent, or at least in need of clarification, redefinition, or correction, as well as by those immediately congenial to them. An understanding of relations between theories of the neoclassical and Romantic periods that may be significant in terms of real intellectual continuity finally depends upon the perception of identities and analogues of basic problem and method between them. Only in the context of such "formative" parallels may similarities and differences of particular concepts and statements of doctrine be reliably interpreted as elements of comparable human *theories,* instead of merely as isolated and incidental similarities and differences of vocabulary and phraseology.[6]

This point may perhaps be clarified by reference to the now quite commonplace observation that the Romantic movement in criticism, especially as illustrated by Coleridge and

---

XXXVIII (1939), 96–106; Lawrence M. Price, "Herder and Gerstenberg or Akenside," *Modern Language Notes,* LXV (1950), 175–78; G. J. ten Hoor, *James Harris and the Influence of his Aesthetic Theories in Germany* (Unpublished dissertation, University of Michigan, 1929); C. F. Weiser *Shaftesbury und das deutsche Geistesleben* (Leipzig and Berlin, 1916); I. C. Hatch, *Der Einfluss Shaftesburys auf Herder* (Breslau, 1901); E. Cassirer, "Schiller und Shaftesbury," *Publications of the English Goethe Society,* XI (1935), 37–59; O. Walzel, *Das Prometheussymbol von Shaftesbury zu Goethe* (2nd ed.; Munich, 1932); H. N. Fairchild, "Hartley, Pistorius, and Coleridge," *PMLA,* LXII (1947), 1010–21; H. von Stein, *Die Entstehung der neueren Ästhetik* (Stuttgart, 1886).

5 See above, Chapter VI, pp. 177–80.

6 For a discussion of an especially striking illustration of the use of absolutely identical terminology and isolated statements of doctrine about a generally common subject in the construction of fundamentally different kinds of theories, see "Akenside and Addison: The Problem of Ideational Debt," *Modern Philology,* LIX (1961), 36–48. For several illustrations both of this kind of phenomenon and of its opposite (basically identical principles or doctrines expressed in radically different terminology) see McKeon, "Imitation and Poetry," in *Thought, Action, and Passion,* pp. 102–221, esp. pp. 108–41, 155–73.

the German writers who influenced him, involved a radical shift from the "mechanistic" and "imitative" conceptions of poetic invention characteristic of the neoclassical period to a predominance of "organismic" and "expressive-creative" conceptions. The question is not whether this observation is historically sound (it clearly is, in a general sense); the question is whether the subject can be meaningfully and reliably discussed only on the basis of characteristic terms (or "metaphors") and of isolated statements of doctrine or opinion about "invention," "genius," or "imagination." There were, for example, some exceptional instances in the eighteenth century of the positive use of images of growing plants (of "vegetative" life) in discussions of poetry and poetic production which may be treated as significant "anticipations" of the dominant tendency of Romantic theory.[7] It is unlikely on the face of things, however, that merely from their common use of such images we could demonstrate a real theoretical continuity between the essentially rhetorical approach of Pope or Young [8] or the causal-empirical approach of Alexander Gerard [9] and the dialectical approach of Coleridge—although we

---

[7] Abrams (*The Mirror and the Lamp*, pp. 167–77, 198–201) finds such significant "vegetative" metaphors in Addison, Pope, Edward Young, and Alexander Gerard, among others.

[8] There is no satisfactory analysis, in the problematic manner, of Pope's criticism, but I hope to turn to that project myself in the near future. The notion that Young's doctrines of "originality" in subject matter are a radical "Romantic" departure from the norm of neoclassical rhetorical theory is, I believe, unfounded.

[9] *Essay on Genius* (1774); see W. J. Hipple, Jr., *The Sublime, the Beautiful, and the Picturesque in Eighteenth-Century British Aesthetic Theory* (Carbondale, Illinois, 1957), for a careful and incisive analysis of Gerard's "system." Interestingly enough, Gerard made non-dialectical use of a number of ideas which seem to be drawn most immediately from Akenside. See, e.g., *Essay on Genius*, Part I, Sect. iii, "How Genius Arises from the Imagination": "When a person starts the first hint of a new invention and begins to meditate a work either in art or science, his notion of the whole is generally but imperfect and confused. When a number of opposite conceptions are collected, various views of their connections open to him and

may be certain that he had read these writers with care.

The dialectical theories of the neoclassical period, on the other hand, offer instructive instances of legitimately "creativist" and "organismic" conceptions of poetic invention which bear important similarities, in thematic and methodological ways, to Coleridge's conception but were formulated in terms primarily of "reflection" or "imitation," "association," "mechanism," and "invention and disposition." For Shaftesbury, Akenside, Hartley, and Harris, the universe itself is an organic, "creative" whole, in a comprehensive metaphysical sense, and the special parallels between human and divine art on which these writers all rely involve "organismic" conceptions both of the product of true poetic invention and of the process. The broad analogies involved in these conceptions, however, are not "metaphors"; they are general principles of reasoning by which *all* terms, both literal and metaphorical (if this distinction happens to be relevant at all), may be given precise theoretical significance. Dialectical theories, indeed, are essentially organismic, whatever metaphors they may happen to employ (and they often combine radically different ones),[10] in the sense that just as the divine or comprehensive

perplex his choice. But by degrees the prospect clears." (In *Eighteenth-Century Critical Essays,* ed. Scott Elledge [Ithaca, New York, 1961], II, 892.)

10 There is nothing to prevent anyone from discussing *actual* "biological" or "organic" structures (i.e., plants and animals, or compounds of carbon) in "cartographic," "mimographic," architectural, or even oratorical terms—or a combination of these as Plato himself did (cf. *Timaeus* 48A and *passim*). Certainly, therefore, it is not difficult to use such terms in discussing bodies conceived as essentially *analogous* to biological ones. The analogy to the act of persuasion, by which the universe, the comprehensive animal, came into being, is of course a relatively minor one in Plato's mythic cosmogonical scheme; but there is no reason why it could not have been made a major one. It would seem reasonable, however, to call such analogies "metaphors" only if we know, a priori, the "literal" (i.e., "true") natures of the things which they describe, and thus the "true" meanings of the words employed; but this is at best a dogmatic position for the historian, as historian, to assume. On the other hand, to attempt to recognize basic

whole always precedes and gives meaning, value, or reality to all the parts or elements of being (even, as in Hartley's scheme, when skeptical doubts are raised about man's present ability to "comprehend" that whole either rationally or imaginatively) so the better or true poetic product is a whole whose various parts are all "informed"—given their proper meaning, value, and status—by the poet's grasp, rationally, imaginatively, or through inspiration or grace, of a higher truth and order—*natura naturans* as distinct from *natura naturata,* as Coleridge and other dialecticians formulated it.[11] One of the basic general principles of all dialectical poetic theory, in short, is that poems made merely "mechanically" out of common available materials, without the informing and transforming perception of the higher or better reality, are inferior, limited, and even, according to some writers, destructive in their consequences in the world.[12]

In the neoclassical dialectical theories, moreover, God's own creativity is seen as an active process of "maintenance" and continuing development in space and in time; it is not merely the accomplished creation of a "static" whole. And the invention or creation involved in the better kind of poetry is also

---

analogies (in the sense of formal parts of theory) commits the historian only to a "conventional" frame of literal reference, on a largely hypothetical basis, by which it is somewhat easier for him to distinguish between primarily "integrative" and primarily "differential" modes of thought. But ultimately "analogical" reasoning has no necessary or unique relation to the use or non-use of what we commonly call "metaphors" as verbal units of discourse.

11 See "On Poesy or Art," *Works,* ed. Shedd, IV, 332. Cf. Stephen C. Pepper, *The Basis of Criticism in the Arts,* pp. 74–95.

12 It is in part this principle that accounts for Coleridge's distinctions between imagination and fancy and between "poetry" and "poem," his doctrine that the great poet is necessarily also a great philosopher, and his correlative argument that, although all poems are imitations of nature, in the better poems it is an "ideal" nature for the apprehension of which the "esemplastic" power is primarily responsible. See "On Poesy or Art," *Works,* IV, 331–33; *Biographia Literaria,* I, 107, 202 and II, 8–13, 14–16, 18–20.

a dynamic and developing, "forming" process, not merely an "arrangement" of static, unproductive parts. For Shaftesbury, Akenside, and Harris, it may be overtly called an act of imitating the plastic powers and processes by which God created and maintains the universe. For Hartley, poetic invention involves progressive analogical perception or association according to the necessary laws through which God himself is the continuing cause of all human actions, and the poet's potential voluntary imitation of God must involve, God himself willing, the act of contributing to the dynamic providential scheme of the universe as a whole, which leads inevitably to the salvation of mankind.

All four of the neoclassical writers, then, may be said to work out essentially vitalistic, "organismic" frames of reference for the discussion of poetry, in spite of the fact that their characteristic terms are not "biological" ones. And it may be reasonable to suggest that these are truly significant *theoretical* anticipations of Romantic criticism, if any existed. There are, however, crucial differences of special principles, definitions, and doctrines between them and Coleridge's theory, and these are perhaps symbolic, as it were, of a larger difference between the predominant qualities of the criticism of the two periods in general. For example, Coleridge describes the actual production of a concrete work of "poetry" as an organic, creative and teleological process of "growth from within" in a more radical and thoroughgoing sense than can be found in any of the neoclassical theories. Our task remains, nevertheless, to try to describe and explain such differences in the context of the formative causes of theory, not simply to present them as differences of characteristic metaphors, or of incidental opinions about how poets do or ought to work.

Akenside, for example, offers some scattered parallels to Coleridge's use of the growing plant metaphor,[13] and he de-

---

[13] E.g., *The Pleasures of Imagination*, II, 385–90; III, 399–400.

scribes the poet's creative act in part in terms of spontaneous development. But the important fact is that Akenside retains a typically neoclassical *rhetorical* artistic or "technical" view of the mode of existence of the whole concrete poetic product —the combination of "matter" and "manner." According to Akenside, that is, after the poet's own inward creative and expressive "conception" has been finally developed out of the elaborate germinating, blending, and fusing process, it is then, in an act of "mimic skill," given its proper or appropriate "vehicle," by which it becomes an "object ascertained." And what Coleridge, following Schelling, calls the "outward form" of a work of poetry entails for Akenside, even in "better" poems, largely conventional, pre-established modes and media of artistic "embodiment" corresponding to those aspects of literary effort which ancient rhetoricians discussed under the headings of "disposition" and "elocution." Similar technical, and basically rhetorical, conceptions of the existence of the concrete work of human art are found in the other three neo-classical theories, and to whatever extent their accounts of poetic production may be said to approximate or resemble the "Romantic" notion of spontaneous "growth from within" it is confined to the production of the poetic design, conception, or affective subject matter, conceived as separate from, and independent of, its vehicle or manner of expression.[14]

---

14 Shaftesbury's conception of the analogy between dramatic poems of the better sort and the "inward colloquy" approximates Coleridge's conception of "correspondence" or "unity" between progressive outward form and developing inward form, but Shaftesbury's chief vocabulary for poems is political, architectural, and "gymnastic," not botanical, and the question is basically one of employing the "manner" most appropriate to the dialectical subject matter. Hartley, in his "naturalistic" phase, speaks of the mutual influence, according to natural psychological laws, among subject matter, structure, and figurative and metrical language, suggesting one of Coleridge's basic doctrines about the organic status of a work of poetry; but Hartley's characteristic terminology is "physical-psychological" (of the mechanistic-atomistic variety), and the practical issue is one of know-

Coleridge's theory, in contrast, has its special "botanical" organismic dimension also in regard to a dynamic relationship between the "inward form" and the "outward form." [15] But clearly what is fundamental here is not the use of an analogy to plant growth per se; it is the fact that Coleridge tended to view the existential status (so to speak) of human works of art as he did that of natural objects. Works of art, like works of nature, actually exist as concrete material entities, as "physical" things; it is only by human experience, through eyes and ears, of their "outward form" or physical structure that they can have their distinctive effects on men and that they can be known. And ideally the outward form in art comes to be not simply by the artistic embodiment of prior creative inventions (however these may be conceived) in effective or appropriate arrangements and media, conventional or contrived; it comes to be by a process of development from within, as does the outward form of any natural object. The "perfection" of the

---

ing how to provide the most effective expression of the subject matter. Harris defines human art in terms of the "efficient form" without which the various materials of works would remain forever "shapeless," a definition that suggests an important aspect of Coleridge's doctrine of the dependence of the outward form of a work on the poet's subjective forming *power;* but Harris' characteristic language is a combination chiefly of logical and ontological distinctions taken from Aristotle and broadly rationalistic moral topics taken from the Stoics, and he eventually concludes that the efficient forming principle in any human art is always external to its "matter," even in an art like poetry, where the form of mind works upon the matter of mind. It is perhaps important to note also that Shaftesbury and Harris, like the ancient Stoics, tend to conceive the dynamism of the created universe itself chiefly as "cyclical" or a matter of periodic recurrence and replenishment; Hartley and Akenside tend to see it as a "progressive" development. But only Akenside offers anything approximating a "biological" conception of progress in nature (see *Pleasures of Imagination,* II, 240–77; cf. G. R. Potter, "Mark Akenside, Prophet of Evolution," *Modern Philology,* XXIV [1926], 55–64, and A. O. Lovejoy, *The Great Chain of Being* [New York, 1936], pp. 263–65).

15 See "On Poesy or Art," *Works,* IV, 328–29. Cf. "On Style," *ibid.,* p. 343; *Biographia Literaria,* I, 174.

outward form is "one and the same" with the fullness of the development of the inward form.[16]

Coleridge, in other words, rejects the neoclassical rhetorical "artistic" principle in favor of one in which whole concrete products of art are to be examined according to precisely the same laws and processes as the concrete products of nature—a principle characteristic in general of the causal-empirical approach to art.[17] Although the "biological" aspect of Coleridge's approach does indicate a shift from the Democritean "mechanico-corpuscular" definition of objects as structures of primary elements to a more Aristotelian view of the nature of concrete wholes [18] (and there is no doubt that the teleologi-

---

16 "Shakespeare, A Poet Generally," *Works,* IV, 55; "On Poesy or Art," *ibid.,* pp. 332–36. In a very general sense, although all four neoclassical dialecticians would agree with Coleridge that the "inward" form of a poem should always have control over the "outward" form, for them this would mean simply that the "surface qualities" of the "manner," vehicle, mode of expression, or medium of a poem are ultimately less important than the qualities of the subject matter. The distinction is the essentially rhetorical one of the *what* and the *how* (equivalent in general to the modern distinction of "content" and "form")—though *within* the discussion of poetic subject matter special concepts of "form" also appear: Hartley develops a "Democritean" conception of the structure of natural phenomena imitated, and Harris borrows the Aristotelian definition of artistic form as external or separable shaping principle, whereas Shaftesbury and Akenside retain more of the classical rhetorical flavor, concerning themselves with the higher and lower "forms of being" (the *res* rather than the *verba*) to be "discovered" by the poet through rational criticism or imaginative perception.

17 See McKeon, "Imitation and Poetry," *Thought, Action, and Passion,* pp. 113–117. Akenside, of course, also speaks of the "object ascertained" perceived by "eyes and ears" that finally results from the poet's "breathing" his conception into the "proper vehicle"; but he does not treat this objectification as a "natural" process, and he views the importance of the material verbal medium simply in terms of the artistic *content* which it can carry and communicate.

18 He condemns unequivocally the mechanico-corpuscular hypothesis, but he does not give up the reality of physical objects. See "Note on a Passage in the Life of Henry Earl of Morland," *Works,* IV, 327–28; "Hints towards the Formation of a More Comprehensive Theory of Life," *Works,* I, 402–3, 387–88; "Aids to Reflection," *ibid.,* pp. 356–59; *Biographia Literaria,* I, 174–79.

cal and vitalistic idea of a "self-organizing" productive power in the whole of nature reflects something more than a special interest on Coleridge's part in biological imagery),[19] his theory of poetry is not of the quasi-problematic variety such as Harris developed. For when the Aristotelian teleological and vitalistic concepts appear in Coleridge's discussion of human art the basic Aristotelian problematic principles (which are not completely altered in Harris' scheme)—that works of art differ from natural objects because they do not have their own "inner" cause of existence and their perceptible outward matter is not the "natural" matter of the form embodied—are subverted by the un-Aristotelian principle that it is the similarity, rather than the difference, between natural productive processes and those of human creativity that is of basic importance.

"Remember," Coleridge said, "that there is a difference between form as proceeding, and shape as superinduced." [20] But the method of the better kind of art is the method of nature; creative imagination is *coadunative.* [21] In short, central elements of Coleridge's scheme do parallel Aristotle's theory of nature; but the use of the status or mode of existence of natural things as criterion for works of human art distinguishes Coleridge's theory of poetry from Aristotle's (and from Harris' as well as Akenside's) in a fundamental way. The Aristotelian concept of intrinsic efficient and final "forming" causes of concrete wholes may thus be described as a special

---

19 See, e.g., *The Friend*, "Second Section," Essay X, *Works*, II, 448–57. Cf. "Theory of Life," *Works*, I, 373–416. Coleridge was deeply interested in the relatively "new" science of biology, especially as practiced by men like John Hunter (1728–93) and John Abernethy (1764–1831), and he strove to apply vitalistic conceptions even to matter normally considered "inorganic." His turn toward "organicism" in poetic theory obviously cannot be separated from this general interest; but it is only part of the explanation.

20 "On Poesy or Art," *Works*, IV, 336.

21 *The Friend*, "Second Section," Essay IV, *Works*, II, 415. Cf. "Theory of Life," *Works*, I, 387n.

"Romantic" characteristic, as it were, of Coleridge's quasi-causal theory, somewhat as the classical "rhetorical" view of works of art is a special characteristic of all four of the neoclassical theories.

Coleridge's theory is, however, like them, dialectical. The ideal of an organic unity of inward and outward form is justified not merely as something of which human beings happen to be capable, and not merely as resulting in adequate or proper "imitations of nature," but as an analogue of the natural organic creative process, the eternal life and action, which we can discover in the physical universe as a whole; and thus from the point of view of actual differences of *theory* the contrast between the neoclassical dialecticians' and Coleridge's discussions of poetic invention may best be explained as divergences of special principles and definitions within the framework of their common dialectical concern with the analogy between human and divine creation.

To state the issue in very general terms, the differences of specific doctrines of organic unity and of the nature and relation of poetic "matter" and "manner" involve a difference in the amount of emphasis placed on the potential harmony or parallel between the "calculative" or "artistic" aspects of human art—as distinct from the spontaneous or "natural" aspects—and divine creation. As there is no reason, according to the neoclassical dialectician, why God's creativity must be considered as involving spontaneous development or "growth" of form in matter, as distinct from the deliberate exertion of forming power from without, so there is no reason why we must concentrate primarily on the spontaneous aspects of human production when we consider it analogous to divine creation. In Coleridge's theory, although it is the facts of human reflection, freedom, and choice which distinguish human art in general from the "wisdom" of nature,[22] the posi-

---

22 "On Poesy or Art," *Works*, IV, 332.

tive analogy between human and divine creativity (by which better works of human art are distinguished from worse) centers chiefly on what may be called "natural" processes of creation rather than "artistic" ones. In true poetry that "synthetical and magical power, to which we have exclusively appropriated the name of imagination" and which is a "dim Analogue of Creation," [23] subordinates art to nature as well as the "manner" to the "matter," [24] and this reflects Coleridge's special conception of the process or act of divine creativity which the human poet may be said to imitate positively. Human imagination, Coleridge says, is an analogue not of "all that we can believe" of Creation, but of "all that we can conceive." [25] We can *believe* that the universe as a whole exists because of the imposition by God of an active form "from without," and even that there was a time when noth-

[23] Letter to Richard Sharp, 15 January 1804 (*Collected Letters*, II, 1034). There is an ambiguity here, apparently produced by Coleridge's vacillation about how strongly to emphasize the analogy between human and divine creativity. Shawcross notes that according to Sara Coleridge the sentence in Chapter XIII of *Biographia Literaria* containing the phrase "as a repetition in the finite mind of the eternal act of creation in the the infinite I AM" was "stroked out in a copy of the *B. L.* containing a few marginal notes of the author." I am inclined to think Coleridge's reasons were not primarily theoretical, since the general principle appears in many other places before and after 1817. (See "On Poesy or Art," *Works*, IV, 332–33; "On the Prometheus of Aeschylus" [1825], *ibid.*, pp. 354–65, esp. p. 359; "Confessions of an Inquiring Spirit," *Works*, V, 578; "Aids to Reflection," *Works*, I, 235–36). Though the term *repetition* is perhaps a source of theoretical difficulty, it is not in Coleridge's scheme necessarily incompatible with the term *analogue*. See below, note 31. In Coleridge's later years, in part because his interests have moved more toward metaphysical and theological problems per se, he is more concerned with understanding and reason than with fancy and imagination, but this indicates no very basic change of philosophical principles or method, and he does not abandon the concept or term *imagination* in reference to poets (see "Table Talk" [January 1 and June 23, 1834], *Works*, VI, 496–97, 517–19).

[24] *Biographia Literaria*, II, 12.

[25] Letter to Richard Sharp (*Collected Letters*, II, 1034).

ing existed,[26] but all that we can *conceive* is an organic "union and interpenetration" [27] of the various parts of creation and the *inseparability* of this living creation from its eternal vital cause.[28] If we "could see the divine thought which is present, at once in the whole and every part," visible nature "would give us the impression of a work of art." [29] But we cannot "see" that thought, and so it is not possible to know (in the sense of human scientific understanding) that human poetic creation is an analogue of the "art" by which nature herself was produced.[30] Coleridge thus reveals a stronger tendency than we find among most neoclassical dialecticians to limit the "creative" processes of human poetic production to an analogy to the divine creative processes manifest in nature. And here perhaps is the real key to the meaning of his well-known distinction between "poetry" and "poem" and his tendency to treat the concepts of "poetry" and "poet" as essentially inseparable ones.

But it should be noted that the crucial distinction between conceiving and believing (like that between understanding and reason which Coleridge borrows from Jacobi and Kant) is actually a modification of Hartley's own distinction between comprehension and faith, and it reflects Coleridge's retention, in his "post-Hartley" years, of certain basic features of Hartley's dialectical system, including the general reluc-

---

26 See, e.g., *The Friend*, "Second Section," Essay XI, *Works*, II, 464, 470–71. Cf. "Confessions of an Inquiring Spirit," *Works*, V, 578, where the "transcendent I AM" is described as the ground or substance *in* whom "*is* whatever *verily* is," as distinct (but not separate) from the "Triune God" *by* whom whatever exists does *substantially* exist.

27 *The Friend*, "Second Section," Essay IV, *Works*, II, 416.

28 See *The Friend*, "Second Section," Essay XI, *Works*, II, 466–70.

29 "On Poesy or Art," *Works*, IV, 330.

30 Cf. "Theory of Life," *Works*, I, 384–85n.; "On the Constitution of the Church and State," *Works*, VI, 30–31. On the differences and relations among the faculties of understanding, reason, instinct, and faith, see esp. "Aids to Reflection," *Works*, I, 225–67, 367–72; "Essay on Faith," *Works*, V, 557–65. Cf. "Confessio Fidei," *ibid.*, pp. 15–18.

tance to analogize human poetic production to the "original" divine act of making but the insistence, nevertheless, on taking the theme of imitation of the divine creation observable in nature seriously. And it is, broadly speaking, the same level of "fallen" nature at which, in Hartley's hierarchy, human art is discussed in terms of the mechanism of association and of copying "actual" phenomena. Coleridge *observes,* however, as Shaftesbury, Akenside, and Harris (as well as Immanuel Kant) do but Hartley does not, that human beings have an innate "active" and "creative" forming power by which the "aggregated" phenomenal materials of experience and fancy may be given a higher, nobler meaning, value, and mode of being. It is not surprising that he finds this power analogous to the divine creative power manifest in nature as a whole, just as Hartley found that the human processes of mechanical association and imitation could be made to concur with the higher divine laws and processes by which the universe is properly controlled and guided toward its ultimate state.

Man, of course, is also a part of nature; he is, indeed, at the "head" of the visible creation.[31] Thus it is not surprising,

---

31 "On Poesy or Art," *Works,* IV, 332; *The Friend,* "Second Section," Essay X, *Works,* II, 449–50. Thus one of the principal—and symbolic—ambiguities in Coleridge's philosophy lies in his combination of the ideas of "analogue of" and "participation in." It is an ambiguity in part because he insists on the reality of common physical or material existence but conceives the whole of nature in its higher sense as a mental or spiritual (subjective) one. In a legitimately causal philosophy to be a *part* of nature is simply to behave according to the natural laws, and whether the processes manifest in that behavior are *analogous* to the natural causes which produce it would not be a particularly important question. In a dialectical philosophy, however, the higher perspective is one in which all things are "mutually" identical, or are "substantial" analogues of one another, under a controlling idea, vision, or agency. This ambiguity is for the most part resolved by Coleridge's comprehensive principle of creative reconciliation of the opposites of mind or spirit and mattter in both nature and human art (see "On Poesy or Art," *Works,* IV, 332–33; *Biographia Literaria,* I, 174–94)—a principle which, in a general sense, he shares with Shaftesbury, Akenside, and Harris, but not with Hartley.

either, that Coleridge did not develop a conception of special divine *inspiration* in poets, even in the ambiguous way in which Shaftesbury and Akenside did. The central reason is perhaps similar to that which Harris expresses—inspiraton would be a superfluous concept because of the principle of the original congeniality of vital or formative "ideas" between man and creative nature that exists to be developed and heightened by man himself.[32] "Man" is at the head of the visible creation, and the distinction between the minds of poets and those of men in general is one of degree and mode of operation, not of kind.

But Coleridge's ultimate view of the relation between human and divine mentality retains much of the kind of fideistic emphasis that pervades the second volume of Hartley's work, and this involves recognition of the basic discrepancy between man "as he is" and the "divine" humanity. In this more exalted context, the analogy between human and divine creativity is finally allowed to coalesce with the themes of divine communication and knowledge of true reality in the "symbol" of Christ the Logos:

For Coleridge's attempt to distinguish "analogy," "metaphor," and "symbol," see "Aids to Reflection," *Works*, I, 235–36, 270n.; "Theory of Life," *ibid.*, pp. 399–400; analogy is distinguished from metaphor as "literal use" from "figurative," and analogy is the material or substantial *ground* of symbolic expressions. The divine reconciliation of opposites of matter and spirit in nature and in Christ as Logos is a *literal fact*, and thus the poetic imagination may be viewed as an *analogue* of divine creation in the sense that the process is substantially the same, though "with a difference," whereas to argue that God creates *as man does* would be to confuse a similarity (one that is possibly useful for illustration) with an essential identity—a metaphor or similitude with an analogy. Cf. Coleridge's "literally" analogical scheme of the scale of creation as a whole, "Aids to Reflection," *ibid.*, pp. 180–81, and "Theory of Life," *ibid.*, pp. 373–416. See also "Notes on Jeremy Taylor," *Works*, V, 224.

32 "On Poesy or Art," *Works*, IV, 332–33. Cf. "Theory of Life," *Works*, I, 411–12; "Aids to Reflection," *ibid.*, pp. 351–66; "Confessions of an Inquiring Spirit," *Works*, V, 577–623, esp. pp. 611–18; "Confessio Fidei," *ibid.*, p. 15.

Meditate on the nature of a being whose ideas are creative, and consequently more real, more substantial than the things that, at the height of their creaturely state, are but their dim reflexes; and the intuitive conviction will arise that in such a being there could exist no motive to the creation of a machine for its own sake; therefore, the material world must have been made for the sake of man, at once the highpriest and representative of the Creator, as far as he partakes of that reason in which the essences of all things coexist in all their distinctions yet as one and indivisible. But I speak of man in his idea, and as subsumed in the divine humanity, in whom God loved the world. . . . Yea (saith an enlightened physician), there is but one principle, which alone reconciles the man with himself, with others, and with the world; which regulates all relations, tempers all passions, gives power to overcome or support all suffering, and which is not to be shaken by aught earthly, for it belongs not to the earth; namely, the principle of religion, the living and substantial faith *which passeth all understanding*, as the cloud-piercing rock, which overhangs the stronghold of which it had been the quarry and remains the foundation. This elevation of the spirit above the semblances of custom and the senses to a world of spirit, this life in the idea, even in the supreme and godlike, which alone merits the name of life, and without which our organic life is but a state of somnambulism; this it is which affords the sole sure anchorage in the storm, and at the same time the substantiating principle of all true wisdom, the satisfactory solution of all the contradictions of human nature, of the whole riddle of the world. This alone belongs to and speaks intelligibly to all alike, the learned and the ignorant, if but the heart listens. For alike present in all, it may be awakened, but it can not be given. But let it not be supposed, that it is a sort of knowledge: no! it is a form of BEING, or indeed it is the only knowledge that truly *is*, and all other science is real only so far as it is symbolical of this. The material universe, saith a Greek philosopher, is but one vast complex *mythus*, that is, symbolical representation, and mythology the *apex* and complement of all genuine physiology. But as this principle can not be implanted by the discipline of logic, so neither can it be excited or evolved by the arts of rhetoric. For it is an immutable truth, that what comes from the heart, that alone goes to the heart; what proceeds from a divine impulse, that the godlike alone can awaken.[33]

"Echoes" of all four of the neoclassical dialecticians in this passage should be unmistakable, but viewed in terms of the total canon of his writings (though many of the special principles, definitions, and doctrines are significantly different) Coleridge's dialectic remained throughout his career of the same general quasi-causal variety as Hartley's—a combination primarily of what Coleridge himself called "empirical" science (initially involving a thoroughgoing "mechanistic" approach, later a more "organismic" approach both to "empirical psychology" and to "natural science") and a comprehensive fideistic theology and cosmology in relation to which human experience and action may be given their true meaning and value. The central conception of the active and creative "powers of imagination," which marks his departure from the specific dialectical principles and doctrines of Hartley, does argue strongly that Akenside was important to him in suggesting the direction to be taken in the dialectical scheme which he eventually worked out; and there is no question but that the thought of the later Coleridge comes closer, in general, to the activist emphases of both Shaftesbury and Harris than the largely passivist fideism of Hartley. Still, in Coleridge's theory of poetry the technical and practical rhetorical conceptions and concerns which were of primary importance to Shaftesbury and Akenside, and the special problems, for example, of differentiating methodically the

---

33 *The Friend*, "Second Section," Essay XI, *Works*, II, 466, 471–72. See *ibid.*, pp. 466–68 for Coleridge's conception of the necessary principle of "intervention" in nature; and cf. his doctrines of the Elect, Original Sin, and Redemption in "Aids to Reflection," *Works*, I, 207–225, 229–41, 262–91.

forms or species of human art and literature which occupied the "Aristotelian" Harris, are subordinated to the larger problem of analyzing natural human behavior, as they had been by Hartley, as well as to the comprehensive grasp of the whole of creation in its true being. His eventual rejection of the Hartleian system was produced by his conclusion that the two parts as Hartley presented them did not really hang together, not by any new decision that two parts or forces are not needed; [34] and his turn toward a "biological" kind of "organicism" in natural science as a whole and in empirical psychology and poetic theory, whatever his immediate documentary sources of these ideas might have been, was part of his general attempt to find a way in which natural "behavior" and true creative "action" could be reconciled. With respect to poetry and poems the final solution is expressed not in a positive analogy between human art and what we may believe about the original act of divine creation, or in an analogy, justified by special grace, to God's act of providing for the welfare of mankind, but in the conception of the natural, finite power of imagination as parallel to the eternal act—the continuing divine action—of creation in the universe. It is a solution which resembles in many ways Hartley's own conception of the "necessary" processes of the human mind, but it is framed in terms of innate human spirituality and creative power such as Hartley himself could not reasonably be expected to employ in his pious disquisition on the ruins of our first paradise.

Coleridge offers a singularly clear example of the energetic

---

34 See *Biographia Literaria*, I, 84. See *The Friend*, "Second Section," Essay IX, *Works*, II, 442–48, for Coleridge's "reconciliation" of Bacon and Plato. Cf. the treatment of Aristotle and Plato in *Philosophical Lectures*, ed. K. Coburn (London, 1949), pp. 170–96, esp. pp. 185–95. Two recent essays by other scholars tend to corroborate this view: Richard Haven, "Coleridge, Hartley, and the Mystics," *Journal of the History of Ideas*, XX (1959), 477–94; and Benjamin Sankey, "Coleridge and the Visible World," *University of Texas Studies in Literature and Language*, VI (1964), 59–64.

and resourceful dialectician confronting, rejecting, adopting, modifying, and shaping the various materials of other theories, dialectical and non-dialectical, in a continuing effort to solve the problems which were "naturally" compelling to him—in much the same way as he says the true poet modifies and transforms by creative imagination the materials of fancy, thus reconciling the most fundamental natural "opposites" of human life. Why these problems should have been compelling to him at all is a separate, and perhaps unanswerable, question, but in dialectical schemes the final line between the esemplastic powers of the true poet and those of the true philosopher of poetry is often very thin indeed.

The generalization that the Romantic movement in criticism amounted to a reversal, around the beginning of the nineteenth century, of "the basic orientation of all aesthetic philosophy," [35] although probably too strong, is not wholly erroneous. But when our focus is not merely on general critical topics or subject matter but on actual theory, and our approach to theory is not merely terminological or doctrinal but problematic and methodological in the manner of the present essay, the Romantic movement may be viewed not only as a reversal of the dominant tendencies of the previous age but also as a continuation and triumph of a form of theory that had always been present in English criticism. The significant fact is that a majority of the important critics of the nineteenth century approached the poet and his work by means of the same general disjunctive and analogical kind of reasoning and in terms of the same general "ultimatic" themes which tend to distinguish the theories of Shaftesbury, Akenside, Hartley, and Harris from the majority of their own contemporaries. Although this has not been a discussion of origins or influences, it is not unreasonable to suggest that the development of the kind of Romantic theorizing which Cole-

---

[35] Abrams, *The Mirror and the Lamp,* p. 69.

ridge exemplifies owes something to methodological and thematic antecedents in England in the neoclassical period as well as to the various German influences that have commonly been cited, and that Shaftesbury, Akenside, Hartley, and Harris may be important, if not central, figures in the story.

Index